Spinalonga
Malia
Elounda
Vai
Moni Toplou
Sitia
sithiou
Agios Nikolaos
Mohlos
Lato
Dikteon Andron
Panagia Kera
Orno
Zakros Palati
k t i
Gournia
Thriptis
EASTERN CRETE
Makrygialos
Ierapetra

TWINPACK Crete

DES HANNIGAN

AA Publishing

If you have any comments or suggestions for this guide you can contact the editor at *travelguides@TheAA.com*

How to Use This Book

KEY TO SYMBOLS

- Map reference
- Address
- Telephone number
- Opening/closing times
- Restaurant or café
- Nearest bus route
- Nearest riverboat or ferry stop
- Driving directions
- Facilities for visitors with disabilities
- Other practical information
- Further information
- Tourist information
- Admission charges: Expensive (over €4), Moderate (€2–€4), and Inexpensive (under €2)
- Major Sight
- Minor Sight
- Walks
- Drives
- Shops
- Entertainment and Activities
- Restaurants

This guide is divided into four sections

• Essential Crete: An introduction to the island and tips on making the most of your stay.

• Crete by Area: We've broken the island into four areas, and recommended the best sights, shops, activities, restaurants, entertainment and nightlife venues in each one. Suggested walks and drives help you to explore.

• Where to Stay: The best hotels, whether you're looking for luxury, budget or something in between.

• Need to Know: The info you need to make your trip run smoothly, including getting about by public transport, weather tips, emergency phone numbers and useful websites.

Navigation In the Crete by Area chapter, we've given each area its own colour, which is also used on the locator maps throughout the book and the map on the inside front cover.

Maps The fold-out map accompanying this book is a comprehensive map of Crete. The grid on this fold-out map is the same as the grid on the locator maps within the book. The grid references to these maps are shown with capital letters, for example A1; those to the town plan are shown with lower-case letters, for example a1.

Contents

Introducing Crete

Crete is like a country in its own right—essentially Greek, yet emphatically Cretan, a destination that captivates with its compelling archaeological sites and museums, spectacular landscapes, vibrant cities and resorts and some of the finest beaches.

Geography is what defines Crete. It is the largest island in Greece and the fifth largest island in the Mediterranean. It lies far to the south of mainland Greece, its one face turned towards Europe, the other towards Africa. The island's dramatic history is written across the colourful fabric of a landscape that embraces snow-capped mountains and rugged coast, forests and olive groves, timeless villages, cosmopolitan cities and lively beach resorts. It is a landscape signposted by the ruins of the palaces and towns of a Bronze Age Minoan civilization that began in 3,000BC.

Crete's later influences came from Arab, Roman, Venetian and Ottoman occupation, while recent history saw the islanders resist, with vigour and self sacrifice, the short-lived occupation by German forces in the 1940s. Such a complex and vivid history, together with Crete's own powerful Greekness, its religious, folklore and musical traditions, creative crafts and cuisine, sets the island apart.

Today, Crete thrives under the Aegean sun, sometimes frustrating in the hot, hectic streets of bustling modern towns and cities, sometimes almost too big and varied to take in at a glance. Yet always there is a peaceful escape into the cool enclaves of the old Venetian quarters of Chania and Rethymno and to the serene peace and quiet of mountainside and monastery, wild coast and wooded valley. Crete's very size and complexity imparts a rare sense of belonging, even to the casual visitor and, if you are willing to explore, there are a hundred different Cretes waiting to enchant you. Above all, the people of Crete, whether in their busy, boisterous cities and resorts or in their often remote mountain eyries, know the meaning of *filoxenia* (kindness to strangers) in a profound and enduring way.

Facts + Figures

- **Crete is the most southerly region of Greece.**
- **Crete has 1,046km (649 miles) of coastline.**
- **The highest point of the island is Mount Psiloritis at 2,456m (8,057ft).**

WHAT'S IN A NAME

Crete's name may derive from *kreti*, a Sanskrit word for creation. But during the Venetian era the island was known as Candia, the Italian for the Arabian name Khandak, meaning ditch; a reference to the defensive ditch excavated round ninth-century Iraklio by Andalucian Arabs.

CRADLE OF THE GREAT GOD

The God Zeus was born on Crete. His pregnant mother, Rhea, fled to the island having already had five of her babies eaten by her husband Cronus, who was terrified of being overthrown by one of his offspring. Two of Crete's many caves lay claim to being the birthplace of Zeus. One is the Ideon Cave (▷ 80) on the slopes of the island's highest mountain, Psiloritis. The other is the Dikteon Cave (▷ 98), high on the Lasithiou Plateau in the east of the island.

THE BEAUTIFUL PEOPLE

The most intriguing of Crete's historical peoples are the Bronze Age Minoans, whose culture expressed itself in sophisticated palaces and good living. We have no proven idea what these 'beautiful people' were called. The Minoan moniker derived from the mythical King Minos of Crete and was conjured up by Sir Arthur Evans, who excavated the Minoan palace of Knossos (▷ 76–77) in the early 1900s.

A Short Stay in Crete

DAY 1: IRAKLIO

Morning Start the day with a visit to the hectic and cheerful market street of Odos 1866, just south of **Platia Venizelou** (▷ 31) and across the busy Dikeosinis. Retrace your steps to the Platia.

Mid-morning Have coffee at **Corner Café** (▷ 35) in Platia Venizelou, where you will see all of Iraklio pass by, and where everything from festivals to political rallies take place. After coffee, stroll along Odos Dedalou, the modern shopping street of Iraklio, and into the open and sunny Platia Eleftherias. Visit the flagship **Archaeological Museum** (▷ 24–25) for a feast of Minoan art and culture.

Lunch Follow Doukos Bofor and on to Odos Epimenidou for lunch at the quirky **Café Veneto** (▷ 35).

Afternoon Head down to the harbour and visit the Venetian-era **Koules Fortress** (▷ 26). If you still feel able for a *post prandial* walk, stride out along the harbour mole and back and then follow the seafront west along Odos Sofokli Venizelou. Cross the busy road (with care) to reach the **Historical Museum of Crete** (▷ 27). If you have time, recross the road and turn left to reach the **Natural History Museum** (▷ 28–29) in its waterside building.

Dinner For some inventive Cretan cuisine try **Parasies** (▷ 36), a few metres away from the Historical Museum, or head back into town to **Peri Orexeos** (▷ 36).

Evening Back in Iraklio, head to **Pagopoeion** (▷ 35) for some cool jazz or to the **Kazantzakis Theatre** (▷ 35) for an evening of classical music or dance.

DAY 2: RETHYMNO

Morning Catch the bus to **Rethymno** (▷ 50–51) from Iraklio's bus station A. From Rethymno stretch your legs along the seashore road and on round the headland, beneath the walls of the Fortezza (Venetian Fortress) to reach the town's attractive Venetian Harbour. Stop for coffee at the popular **Café Nuvel** (▷ 66), overlooking the Venetian Harbour.

Mid-morning Retrace your steps, following the **Rethymno walk** directions (▷ 61) to visit the **Archaeological Museum** (▷ 56). From the museum its only a few steps to the **Fortezza** (▷ 56), but leave this for later, as it remains open throughout the day.

Lunch Enjoy an early lunch at the Marina Restaurant (€), just down from the Archaeological Museum.

Afternoon After lunch follow the walk directions through the narrow streets of the old town. The route takes you past the **Neratzies Mosque** (▷ 65). Just before the mosque divert along Odos Vernadou to visit the **Historical and Folk Museum** (▷ 57). Follow the rest of the directions, making sure to linger along the narrow street of Soulou where there are several quirky shops. At the waterfront and from the Venetian Harbour head back along Kefalogiannidon and up the steps, to visit the Fortezza.

Dinner For an early dinner choose between the cheerful **To Pigadi** (▷ 68) or the long-established **Avli** (▷ 66), both are located in narrow Odos Xanthoudidou.

Evening Back in Iraklio, enjoy a nightcap in one of the café–bars in **Platia Venizelou** (▷ 31) or Odos Handakos.

Top 25

➤➤➤

Agia Triada ▷ 72 Minoan palace, thought to have been the summer home of nearby Phaistos.

Agios Nikolaos ▷ 90–91 One of the most engaging small towns in Greece with everything you need.

Aptera ▷ 40–41 Greek, Roman, Ottoman and World War II remains make this an archaeological treasure.

Zakros Palati ▷ 96 Ancient Minoa has a powerful presence at these atmospheric ruins.

Sitia ▷ 95 Unwind on Sitia's sweeping promenade with its broad harbour and backdrop of distant mountains.

Rethymno ▷ 50–51 Quirky shops, outstanding restaurants and historic buildings enhance Crete's lively cultural centre.

Phaistos ▷ 78–79 For many visitors, this Minoan site and its superb location, matches Knossos for its appeal.

Panagia Kera ▷ 94 A tiny building whose stunning interior is a feast of ancient icons.

Palaiochora ▷ 52 A south-coast resort that manages to preserve a cheerful village spirit on its sundrenched peninsula.

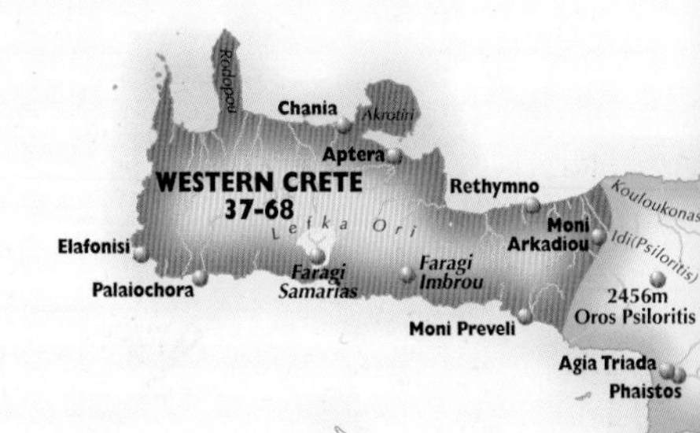

Oros Psiloritis ▷ 80 Pull on your walking shoes for the heartland of Crete's awesome mountains.

Mouseio Fisikis Istorias Kritis ▷ 28–29 Iraklio's waterfront Natural History Museum has everything.

Moni Preveli ▷ 49 A magnificent setting enhances the tranquillity of these ancient buildings.

These pages are a quick guide to the Top 25, which are described in more detail later. Here they are listed alphabetically, and the tinted background shows which area they are in.

Archaiologiko Mouseio ▷ **24–25** Enjoy the world's finest collection of breathtaking Minoan artefacts.

Chania ▷ **42–43** Venetian Chania, its beautiful harbour and enchanting old town, will win your heart.

Cretaquarium ▷ **73** The Mediterranean's sea creatures welcome you to this prestigious aquarium.

Elafonisi ▷ **44** Think tropical at this swathe of sunkissed beaches and shallow, crystal-clear water.

Elounda and Spinalonga ▷ **92** This most desirable resort features a peninsula and offshore island.

Enetiko Limani and Frourio Koules ▷ **26** Iraklio's eyecatching fortress.

Faragi Imbrou ▷ **45** Escape the crowds in this canyon, smaller but equally as thrilling as Samaria's.

Faragi Samarias ▷ **46–47** A beast of a gorge and an amazing place to be.

Gortys ▷ **74–75** Ancient history lies scattered across the landscape at this post-Minoan site.

Istoriko Mouseio ▷ **27** This splendid musuem in Iraklio brings to life the dramatic history and culture of Crete.

IRAKLIO
Archaiologiko Mouseio
Enetiko Limani & Frourio Koules
Istoriko Mouseio
Mouseio Fisikis Istorias Kritis

Moni Arkadiou ▷ **48** A sense of a dramatic and often tragic past surrounds this iconic monastery.

Lasithiou Plateau ▷ **93** Take the spiral road into the Dikti Mountains to reach this flat and fertile corner.

Knossos ▷ **76–77** Crete's flagship archaeological site, often crowded, but always compelling.

Out and About

You can soak up the sun on Crete's fabulous beaches, browse the island's world-class museums and ancient sites, while away the hours in cafés and tavernas, or shop 'til you drop; but why not explore the wilder side of Crete instead, on the island's spectacular mountains, rocky coastline and shining sea?

Playful goats; a pelican beside the Almiros River; cherry blossom; wild flowers (top to bottom)

Hundreds of years of human impact, through deforestation, agriculture, animal grazing, hunting and, lately, tourism development, has depleted the wildlife diversity of Crete, an island once covered from end to end with trees. Wide-scale damage began with the Venetians who stripped the island of its natural forests for building its mighty naval fleet. Yet such is Crete's size that human impact is fairly well contained. Today, the island's infrastructure supports a surprising biodiversity that includes more than 1,600 plant species alone. The spring display of blossoms is magnificent at a time when anemones, wild irises, blue campanulas and sixty varieties of orchids are found in abundance, and the famous Judas tree lights up the landscape with its pink flowers.

Colourful Patchwork

Even in early summer the high mountains and areas such as the Lasithiou Plateau (▷ 93) and the Amari Valley (▷ 81) retain their wild flowers for a touch longer, into early June in places. The blistering heat of summer

PROTECTING THE WILD

Many of Crete's wild species have been lost forever and many are still endangered, while a tradition of shooting and trapping on Crete accounts for the deaths of countless wild creatures. The magnificent lammergeir (bearded vulture) is now reduced on Crete to a bare two dozen survivors on the Lasithiou and Omalos plateaus. But anyone visiting Iraklio's Natural History Museum (▷ 28–29) will see reflected there a spirit of growing environmental awareness among Cretans, especially the young.

Steep cliffs rise from the sea; a cistus flower; a watchful goat (top to bottom)

dries up the more barren landscapes of the island to a colourful patchwork of white and orange rock and blood-red earth, where shrubs and herbaceous plants survive and the exquisite aromas of sage, lavender, rosemary and thyme drench the air. In the deep gorges like Samaria (▷ 46–47) and Imbros (▷ 45), where shade and a lingering dampness prevail, there is a wealth of shrubs and late flowering plants. Autumn reinvigorates the parched earth with its cooler nights and damp dawns and soon, the winter rains that keep Crete green at heart arrive.

Birds and Beasts

Over 330 species of birds have been recorded in Crete, including typical Mediterranean residents such as quail, crested lark, stonechat, wheatear, rock thrush and the larger raptors such as buzzard, golden eagle and griffon vulture. In spring, in wetland areas such as Elafonisi (▷ 44), migratory waders, including marsh sandpiper, avocet and wagtail, may be spotted. Many of Crete's wild mammals have been supplanted by the ubiquitous sheep and goats of the uplands. Crete's iconic *kri-kri*, the big horned wild goat (or *agrimi* as it is known by islanders) still survives in the Lefka Ori (White Mountains), however. The mountains support such sizeable wild creatures as badgers, hares and weasels, and a single Cretan wild cat, long thought to be extinct, was recorded in 1996.

ALL AT SEA

The great seas round Crete support dolphins and even sperm whales, while the rare monk seal breeds in remote coastal caves and on some uninhabited islands. One of the Mediterranean's most iconic creatures, the loggerhead turtle *(caretta-caretta)* is known to breed in certain parts of Crete and has strict protection and monitoring. The crystal clear waters around the island are a paradise for divers, and several reliable diving schools cater for beginners and experts alike.

Shopping

Crete's culture and its long reliance on agriculture has left a legacy of distinctive food and drink, clothing, pottery, musical instruments and other objects that can be found in the island's vast range of markets, shops and craft galleries.

Olive oil, Florina peppers and local cheese are sold at the markets; local embroidery (top to bottom)

Market Values

It's in local markets especially where you'll find food products and other goods that are the essence of Crete. Unmissable are the main markets of Iraklio, Chania and Rethymno with everything from freshly caught fish to famous Cretan herbs, honey and cheeses. Weekly markets take place in smaller towns and villages, where you can pick up locally made bags and baskets and even traditional Cretan wear, such as *stivania*, knee-length boots, or the famous *sariki*, a crocheted headscarf fringed with tiny knots.

Catwalk Crete

In Crete's towns, cities and resorts you're more likely to see the influence of the latest chain-store look. But there's also eye-catching fashion on show in the main cities and in resort towns such as Agios Nikolaos. In popular shopping streets such as Iraklio's Dedalou (▷ 34) there are clothes shops boasting top brand names to tempt the fashion conscious, while in Chania's Odos Skridlof, known as Leather Street, you're spoiled for choice when it comes to leather goods. Interspersed with these are numerous jewellery shops.

SOUVENIRS

Most visitors like to take a tangible memory of Crete back home, but you need to be cautious about what you buy, given the possibility of excess baggage fees at airports and security restrictions on what you carry in cabin luggage. Many so-called cheap souvenirs may also be imported. Woven goods, embroidery, olive wood pieces and pottery bought in rural centres or bona fide craft galleries are a good bet.

Crete by Night

Some of Crete's towns and resorts look enchanting under the night sky

Night steals gently across the Cretan landscape, creating a spectacular natural light show as the sun sinks into the western sea or slips behind the mountains. Long before the sun departs, however, towns and resorts glow with artificial light as the evening *volta*, the sociable stroll along quayside and promenade, begins, and the bars and cafés throb with conversation and music before it's time for the evening meal.

Mellow Evenings

In places such as Iraklio sidewalk tables soon fill up, and a delightful mood of relaxation and good nature descends with the dusk. At Chania and Agios Nikolaos and in dozens of resorts, it's the waterside cafés that draw the crowds to muse on life alongside the lapping waters streaked with light reflections. Every Venetian fortress is framed by subtle floodlighting, and the maze of narrow alleyways in villages are pooled with light and shadow.

Music for All

In village taverna and *kafenion* there's the chance of traditional Cretan music soothing the night air or electrifying the mellow darkness. If slow nightlife is not your thing then head for Iraklio (▷ 35) or the resorts such as Malia (▷ 99), where summertime clubs rock into the early hours. In the bigger venues international DJs feature everything from house to R'n'B, rock and retro, while many clubs have Greek rock.

BE SAFE BY NIGHT

Crete is a generally unthreatening place by night, but you should always keep valuables in a secure place about your person rather than in a handbag or satchel. Street lighting can be poor in places, especially in resorts. Potholes in roads and streets, and even road works, are often unprotected and may lack warning signs or lights. When walking between bars and clubs on the outskirts of resorts, keep a sharp eye on traffic.

Eating Out

Cretan cooking starts in the home, especially in villages, where generations of cooks have learned to be creative, not least because of the wealth of wild herbs available. Modern Cretan cuisine has absorbed such traditions and has happily assimilated the culinary styles of other cultures.

There's a Name for It

The focus of Cretan village life is the traditional café, the *kafenion*, still often a male preserve. In the cities, towns and resorts, the modern café, or *kafeteria*, is now the norm and you'll even spot American chain outlets. The ubiquitous Greek taverna still dishes up traditional food such as grilled meat. An *ouzeri* or a *mezedhopolio* specializes in *mezédhes*—starter dishes of meat, seafood, vegetables and cheeses that, collectively, can be a meal in themselves and can often be reasonably priced. Places specializing in fish are known as *psarotavernas,* while an *estiatorio* is a conventional restaurant.

The Time Element

A Cretan breakfast is often a simple coffee and pastry, but for holidaymakers many hotels offer a good buffet breakfast. Lunch can start as late as one or two o'clock in the afternoon and is lingered over. The real meal deal is dinner; Cretans eat in the cool of late evening and meals can go on until midnight. No one stands on ceremony and the dress code is refreshingly relaxed, although in top-end restaurants, diners are increasingly fashion conscious.

COUNTING THE COST

Increasingly Iraklio, Chania, Rethymno, Agios Nikolaos and many resorts and outlying venues boast restaurants whose accomplished chefs create a marvellous fusion of Cretan and international cuisine. The price can be high, but you can still eat well at budget cost in the many simple tavernas or streetside *souvlaki* stalls and fast food outlets found in towns and cities and in most big resorts.

The Ferryman Tavern, Elounda; squid hang outside a roadside restaurant; Cretan appetizers; a tavern in Imbros (top to bottom)

Restaurants by Cuisine

Crete has just about every kind of eatery to suit all tastes, although there is, fortunately, a distinctive Greek and Cretan flavour to the island's tavernas and restaurants. For a more detailed description of each restaurant, see Crete by Area.

BOUTIQUE AND THE BEST

Alana (▷ 66)
Avli (▷ 66)
Brillant/Herb's Garden (▷ 36)
Café Veneto (▷ 36)
Cosmos (▷ 66)
Du Lac (▷ 106)
Ferryman (▷ 106)
Kariatis (▷ 67)
Pagopoeion (▷ 36)
Parasies (▷ 36)
Peri Orexeos (▷ 36)
Safran (▷ 68)
Tamam (▷ 68)
To Pigadi ▷ 68)
Veneto (▷ 68)
Well of the Turk (▷ 68)

CAFÉS AND LIGHT MEALS

Café Nuvel (▷ 66)
Café Platia (▷ 86)
Central Park (▷ 35)
Corner Café (▷ 35)
Gefira (▷ 67)
Gialos (▷ 86)
Ilios Café (▷ 106)
Kyria Maria (▷ 67)
Nostrale (▷ 65)
Utopia (▷ 35)
Zygos (▷ 106)

SEAFOOD

The Blue House (▷ 66)
O Faros (▷ 86)
Ippokampos (▷ 36)
Levante (▷ 106)
Pelagos (▷ 106)
Scala (▷ 86)
Thalassografia (▷ 68)
Tou Terzaki (▷ 36)

TRADITIONAL TAVERNA

Aravanes Taverna (▷ 86)
O Belgou (▷ 86)
Castello (▷ 66)
Creta (▷ 86)
Dionysos (▷ 66)
Giakoumis (▷ 36)
Faka (▷ 66)
Kalesma (▷ 86)
Karnagio (▷ 67)
Mesostrati (▷ 106)
Methexis (▷ 67)
Milia (▷ 67)
Mylos Tou Kerata (▷ 67)
Nikterida (▷ 67)
Palaios Milos (Vieux Moulin) (▷ 68)
Remezzo (▷ 106)
Xani (▷ 68)

If You Like...

However you'd like to spend your time in Crete, these top suggestions should help you tailor your ideal visit. Each suggestion has a fuller write-up elsewhere in the book.

THE ART SCENE

Overdose on Minoan frescoes and pottery at Iraklio's Archaeological Museum (▷ 24–25).
Frame up at such great regional art galleries as those at Rethymno (▷ 50–51), Chania (▷ 42–43) and Agios Nikolaos (▷ 90–91).
Browse the classier gallery shops of Chania and Rethymno (▷ 63–64).

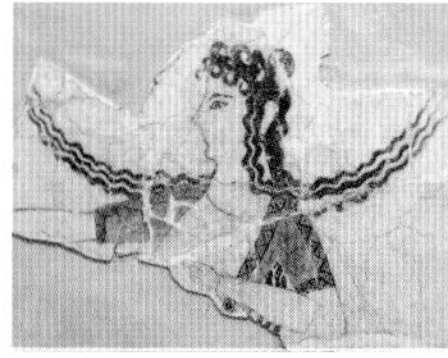

Minoan fresco, Knossos (top); beach bar at Limin Hersonisos, Malia (above)

BEING ON THE WATER

Board one of the ferries (▷ 117) that link the south-coast ports.
Hop off Crete and get a boat from Palaiochora (▷ 52) to the fascinating island of Gavdos.
Get wet windsurfing or settle for a pedalo; Diros Beach Watersports (▷ 105) can oblige.
Try a moonlit cruise from Agios Nikolaos with Nostos Boat Trips (▷ 105).

THE BUDGET BONUS

Study Crete's bus timetables for great ways of getting about (▷ 118).
Munch a local's lunch at the tavernas serving the big markets of Iraklio (▷ 34), Chania and Rethymno (▷ 64).
Check for dual discount tickets covering museums and ancient sites (▷ 25, 53, 54, 77).

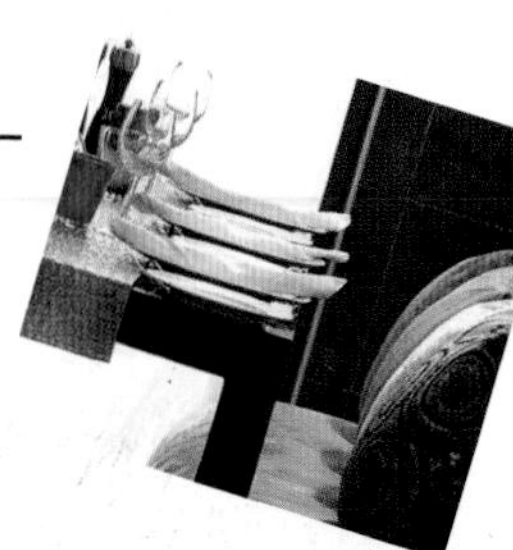

CAFÉ SOCIETY

Harbourside ease is the rule at Rethymno's Café Nuvel (▷ 66).
People-watch at Iraklio's Corner Café (▷ 35), Platia Venizelou.
Stop the World at Zygos Café (▷ 106) in Agios Nikolaos.

Greek salad (above right); the Brilliant restaurant at the Lato Hotel, Iraklio (right)

Herb's Garden, Iraklio

Local embroidery

CRETAN CUISINE

For the finest food in stylish surroundings head for Iraklio's Brillant (▷ 36), its summer sister Herb's Garden (▷ 36), or Rethymno's Veneto (▷ 68).

Go fishing for the best seafood at Agia Galini's O Faros (▷ 86).

Good-value taverna dining is a certainty at the friendly Methexis (▷ 67) in Palaiochora.

Taste buds at the ready for great local cooking at tavernas such as The Blue House (▷ 66) in Loutro.

CRETAN MEMORIES

Flavour, aroma and taste make Moni Toplou's (▷ 104) fabled honey the food of the Gods.

Try out a genuine designer hat at Chania's delightful Pantos Kairou shop (▷ 64).

Wrap up your memories in a piece of fine weaving or embroidery from Fodele (▷ 82) or Anogia (▷ 81).

Sink your savings on an expensive replica antiquity from the site shop at Knossos (▷ 84).

FAMILY OUTINGS

Get close to Mediterranean sea life at the amazing Cretaquarium (▷ 73).

Head for family-friendly beaches at Elafonisi (▷ 44) and Makrygialos (▷ 99).

Saddle up for a lovely ride (▷ 85) along beaches or in the mountains.

A freshwater alternative to the beach can be enjoyed by all at Water City (▷ 85).

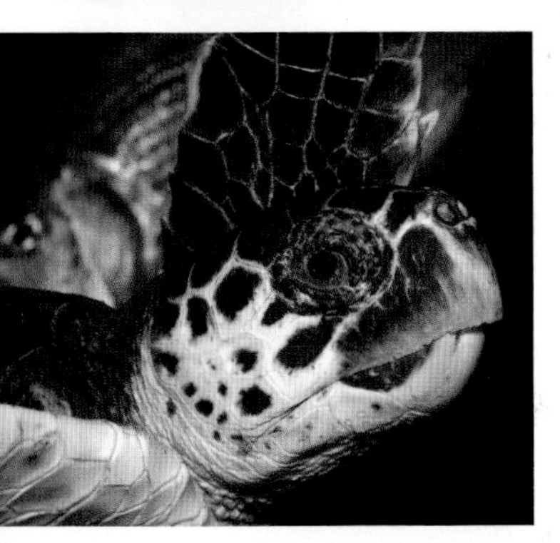

Vases from Iraklio's Archaeological Museum (above left); a resident at Cretaquarium (left)

GOING OFF THE BEATEN TRACK

Trek Samaria (▷ 46), **of course,** but bale out for other great gorges, including Imbros (▷ 45).
Hike the fabulous south coast between Sougia (▷ 58) and Chora Sfakion (▷ 54).

Walking the Imbros Gorge (below)

HOTELS WITH (GREAT) ATTITUDE

Traditional surroundings and modern facilities await at Rethymno's Veneto hotel (▷ 112).
Absolutely quirky and loveable is Chania's creaky old Pension Thereza (▷ 111).
For a thoroughly eco-friendly stay try the old village of Milia (▷ 110).
For comfort and luxury at low prices try Studios Yiorgis (▷ 111) in Palaiochora.

Partying at a resort nightspot (above); restaurants and bars line Lake Voulismeni (below)

PARTYING AND CHILLING OUT

Go over the top (if you must) in the many clubs, discos and music bars of Malia (▷ 99) or on Odos 25 Martiou in Agios Nikolaos (▷ 105).
Chill out in cool bars such as Rethymno's Tholos (▷ 65) or Iraklio's Pagopoeion ▷ 35).
Party on the beach at Matala (▷ 82) or Limin Hersonisos at Malia (▷ 99).

TRIPS THROUGH TIME

Escape the Knossos crowds at the haunting Minoan ruins of Gournia (▷ 98), east of Agios Nikolaos.
Ring the time changes among Aptera's (▷ 40–41) Greek, Roman, Byzantine, Ottoman and World War II remains.
Streetside history is everywhere in Chania (▷ 42–43) and Rethymno (▷ 50–51).
Lose all sense of time at the Archaeological Museums of Iraklio (▷ 24–25), Rethymno (▷ 56), Chania (▷ 53) and Sitia (▷ 95).

Three-part Roman cistern in the ruins at Aptera (right)

Crete by Area

Crete's capital and main port has shaken off its once gritty image and has evolved into a vibrant destination. The city is easy to get around and is crammed with busy cafés, restaurants and shops that complement Iraklio's outstanding museums and historic buildings.

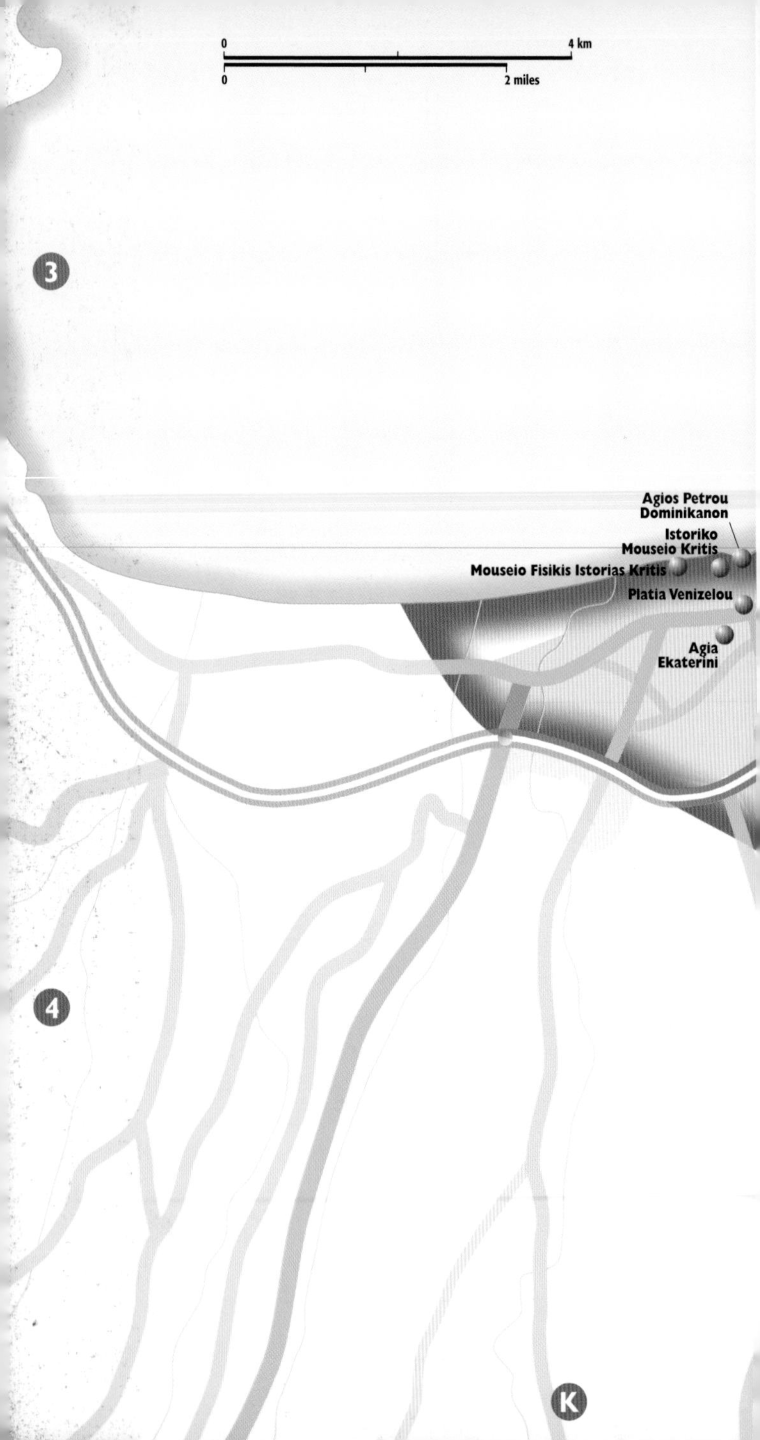

0
4 km
0
2 miles
3
Agios Petrou
Dominikanon
Istoriko
Mouseio Kritis
Mouseio Fisikis Istorias Kritis
Platia Venizelou
Agia
Ekaterini
4
K

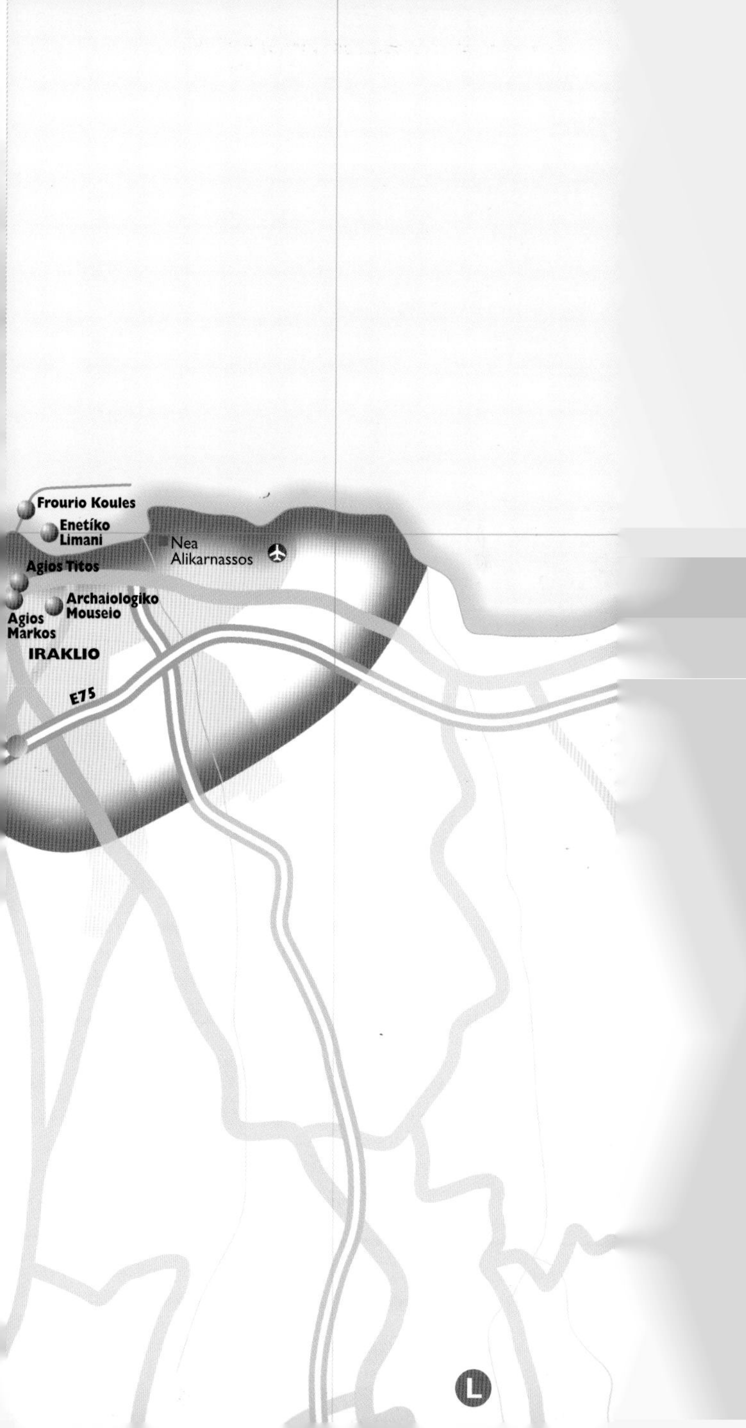
Frourio Koules
Enetíko
Limani
Nea
Alikarnassos
Agios Titos
Archaiologiko
Mouseio
Agios
Markos
IRAKLIO
E75
L

Archaiologiko Mouseio

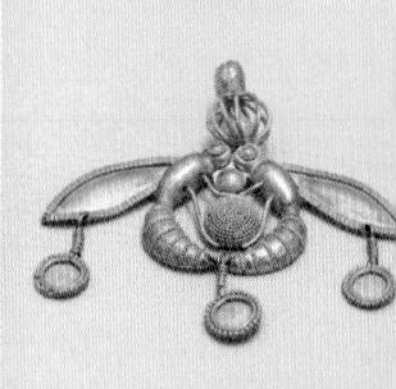

HIGHLIGHTS

- The frescoes
- The King's Gaming Board
- Boar's tusk helmet
- The Phaistos Disc
- The Gold Bee Pendant

TIP

- Be ready to move randomly to less crowded exhibits in a bid to keep one step ahead of the many tour and cruise groups.

Iraklio's Archaeological Museum holds the world's finest collection of Minoan art. Some of the exhibits are so enthralling you feel as if you're the only one there, in spite of the army of fellow visitors.

Vivid collection The museum is undergoing a long drawn out renovation and expansion, scheduled to be fully open by 2012. Viewing is currently limited to a large gallery in the basement of the building. This interim exhibition is well organized, however, and displays some of the museum's finest pieces. There are finds from the Neolithic through to the Roman period, emphasis being on the Minoan era with superb frescoes from the major Minoan sites at Knossos, Phaistos and other settlements throughout Crete. Other artefacts include

Clockwise from far left: Fresco of Priest-King; faïence figurine of a Snake Goddess; fresco of the Bull Leaper; necklaces of gold beads in the shape of papyrus, ivy leaves and confronted argonauts; Zeus-Serapis depicted as Pluto, Lord of the Underworld; gold Bee Pendant from Chrysolakkos

engraved seal stones (used for imprinting clay tablets and wax seals), votive figurines, gold jewellery, weaponry and burial sarcophagi.

Celebratory society The current exhibition brings together the best frescoes from Knossos and date from the high period of Minoan culture, 1600–1450BC. The well-restored frescoes depict a vibrant, celebratory society and include the iconic Bull Leaper, the Prince of the Lilies, and 'La Parisienne', a probable depiction of a priestess, so named because her red lips, wide eyes, long hair and coquettish manner inspired a fanciful comparison to the fashions of 19th-century Europe. Among the equally splendid artefacts are the tiny faïence figures of the bare-breasted Snake Goddesses and the Bull's Head sacred vessel carved from black steatite.

THE BASICS

e3

Platia Eleftherias (temporary entrance on Hatzidakis)

28102 24630

Apr–Oct Mon 1–8, Tue–Sun 8–8; Nov–Mar daily 8–5 (phone to confirm)

Cafés in Platia Eleftherias

Good

Expensive; free on Sun mid-Oct to Mar

Combined ticket available for museum and Knossos (▷ 76–77)

Enetiko Limani and Frourio Koules

Passage to the Fortress (left); the harbour (middle); view from the ramparts (right)

THE BASICS

e1
Enetiko Limani
28102 46211
Mid-Apr to Oct daily 8–6.30; Nov to mid-Apr 8–4.30
Few
Inexpensive (free on Sun Nov–Mar)
When the sea is rough from the west, access to the harbourside approach road and harbour mole is not permitted

HIGHLIGHTS

- Superb views from the ramparts of the Fortress
- The stroll along the harbour mole
- Watching the fishing boats come and go

TIP

- Wear flat-heeled shoes. The sometimes badly-lit, rough stone paving underfoot is not suitable for high heels.

Stroll along Iraklio's sundrenched Enetiko Limani (harbour), then let your echoing footsteps conjure up the ghosts of the past inside the Frourio Koules (Venetian Fortress), the best preserved of Crete's many Venetian fortifications.

Seagoing past Iraklio's sprawling harbour and docks are narrowly separated from the tallest buildings of the city by a veritable torrent of traffic along the waterfront road of Koundourioti. On the city side of the road are the preserved Venetian Arsenals, massive stone vaults that were used for shipbuilding and repair work. The Venetian Fortress is approached along the raised mole above the fishing harbour where *caiques* of all sizes still come and go, saffron-coloured nets are piled high and a clutter of seagoing objects adds an authentic touch.

Echoes of war Built by the Venetians in the 16th century, the Fortress resisted Turkish siege for 21 years. In spite of recent restoration, the eroded honey-coloured stonework of the massive walls is unquestionably ancient, while the rough slabs and cobbles underfoot are polished by centuries of use. The ground floor of the fort is cavernous and empty with only the occasional stone cannonball to signal its military purpose, but there is still a powerful atmosphere. A ramp of rough slabs leads up to the airy battlements, from where there are splendid views of the city, the long harbour mole, the offshore island of Dia and the Psiloritis mountains.

Rear entrance (left); portrait of Nikos Kazantzakis (middle); a reconstruction (right)

Istoriko Mouseio Kritis

There's little chance of museum fatigue at Iraklio's history museum, which is one of the best small museums in Greece. It's filled with colourful displays that outline Cretan history and culture with great flair and fascination.

Absorbing journey The Historical Museum tells the story of Crete from the early Christian era to the 20th century, and occupies the old home of the distinguished Kalokerinos family. The ground floor takes you on a journey through the Byzantine, Venetian and Ottoman periods with a detailed model of Iraklio (then known as Candia) in 1645 putting things in context. Room 2 contains exquisite pottery from all periods including work from the ninth to mid-10th centuries of Andalucian Arab influence. Another room displays sculpture and artefacts from the Basilica of St. Titus at Gortys (▷ 75), while Rooms 6 and 7 cover the Venetian era.

Famous sons The first floor has a reconstructed Byzantine church, and a gallery with work by Crete's famous painter Domenicos Theotokopoulos, El Greco (1541–1614). Other rooms display artefacts from the Ottoman period. The final floor is over two levels, where pride of place goes to another famous Cretan, Nikos Kazantzakis (1883–1957). Rooms 15 and 16 cover the Battle of Crete, and the Occupation and Resistance during World War II, and the second level is devoted to rural life and traditions, with a reconstructed Cretan village home.

THE BASICS

www.historical-museum.gr
d1
Lysimachou Kalokairinou 7 and Sofokli Venizelou 27
28102 83219
Apr–Oct Mon–Sat 9–5; Nov–Mar Mon–Sat 9–1.30
Cafés (€)
Good
Moderate

HIGHLIGHTS

- The Ceramics room on the ground floor
- El Greco's painting of Mount Sinai
- The Nikos Kazantzakis section
- The Rural Life section

TIP

- Walk round to the back of the museum into the narrow Odos Kalokairinou to see the Fountain of Idomeneus, a merging of Venetian and Ottoman features.

Mouseio Fisikis Istorias Kritis

HIGHLIGHTS

- Earthquake Table
- Stavros Niarchos Discovery Centre
- A reconstruction of the enormous Deinotherium, a giant elephant that dates from nine million years ago

TIP

- Check for temporary exhibitions covering a wide range of ecological matters in the museum annexe.

Be shaken, not stirred at this developing museum with an earthquake table that replicates the shocking power of some of the worlds biggest Richter-scale readings; then unwind with the kids at the museum's amazing children's section.

Attractive landmark The University of Crete's Natural History Museum was relocated in 2007 to an old power station on Iraklio's western seafront. An attractive landmark, some of the museum's existing structures have been cleverly incorporated into the refurbished building. The museum is evolving and there is still space for further development of this excellent venue. The ground floor features displays about early mammals and Crete's flora and fauna, while set-piece tableaux show many of the island's

Clockwise from top left: The Natural History Museum stands at the far end of the beach; well-presented displays show animals in their natural habitat; a monk seal display; a nose-horned viper

wild animals past and present, including wolf and wild boar as well as birds and sea creatures.

Earth moving In the basement is the Encelados, an earthquake simulator where you can experience the shock tremors of such infamous upheavals as those of Taiwan in 1999 and Kobi, Japan in 1995. Other sections include a planetarium and a cinema showing environmental films. In the Stavros Niarchos Discovery Centre, the young and the young at heart will find equal fascination with interactive features that include the tiny 'Plane Tree Cinema', the 'Mysterious Cave' and 'A Night at the Campsite'. The museum has a strong emphasis on sustainability and environmental protection, and there is an encouraging promotion of biodiversity and Green issues.

THE BASICS

- c1
- Sofokli Venizelou
- 28102 82740
- Apr–Oct daily 9–9; Nov–Mar Mon–Fri 8.30–3.30, Sat–Sun 10–7
- Café (€)
- Few
- Expensive

More to See

AGIA EKATERINI

The finest collection of icons in all of Greece is housed in Iraklio's Museum of Religious Art at the Church of Agia Ekaterini (St. Catherine). The 15th-century church was part of a monastic school until the end of the Venetian period and many refugee artists from the fall of Byzantium found sanctuary here. Noted practitioners include Mikhail Damaskinos who famously introduced perspective and Italian Renaissance elements into Byzantine iconography. Six of his magnificent works are at the heart of the exhibition. There are enduring claims that Domenico Theotokopoulos, El Greco, was a contemporary of Damaskinos at the School. At the time of writing (2011) the museum was closed but due to open in the near future.

d3 Platia Ekaterinis 28102 88825 Confirm with the TIC (28102 46298-9) Cafés in Platia Ekaterinis Improved access expected after renovation Moderate

AGIOS MARKOS

The Basilica of St. Mark, with its fine arcaded portico, maintains an elegant and restrained presence overlooking Platia Venizelou. Built by the Venetians in 1239 and dedicated to Venice's patron saint, the Basilica is a robust survivor, two of its predecessors having been destroyed by an earthquake, first in 1303 and its successor in 1508. It became a mosque during Ottoman rule, and was then neglected until full restoration (1956–61). Today it is Iraklio's municipal gallery where changing exhibitions of art are staged. The gallery is worth visiting in the evenings when the interior is particularly atmospheric.

d2 Odos 25 Avgoustou 28103 99228 Mon–Fri 9–1.30pm, 6–9 Corner Café (▷ 35) Few Free

AGIOS PETROU DOMINIKANON

The recently renovated Church of Agios Petros lies west of the harbour between the traffic-logged Sofokli Venizelou and Odos I

Agios Titos fronting onto Platia Agiou Titou (▷ 31)

Mitsotaki. The church was built by Dominican monks in the first half of the 13th century and converted into the mosque of Sultan Ibrahim under the Ottomans. The southern chapel preserves the only 15th-century frescoes in Iraklio. Within the grounds are several archaeological excavations. There is no information currently available on the church's future, other than it is expected to re-open to the public in some form.

d1 Odos Sofokli Venizelou Confirm with TIC (28102 46298-9) for information Cafés in the nearby Museum Square

AGIOS TITOS

Originally a Byzantine building and named after the saint who was sent by St. Paul to win Crete for Christianity, various reincarnations of this splendid building were destroyed by earthquakes. After a final rebuilding as a mosque in the Ottoman period, Agios Titos reverted finally to Christian Orthodoxy in 1923. The building is set back in a serene and leafy *platia*. In a small chapel to the left of the entrance porch a reliquary contains the head of St. Titus, much revered by the faithful.

e2 Platia Agiou Titou/Odos 25 Avgoustou 28103 46221 Mon–Sat 8–12, 5–7 Cafés in Platia Agiou Titou Few Free Dress modestly and keep a low profile during services

PLATIA VENIZELOU

This bustling pedestrianized *platia* is the heart of Iraklio; its focal point is the Venetian Morosini Fountain, known also as the Lions' Fountain because of the carved lions that support a large basin at the apex. The fountain dates from 1628, although the lions date from a 14th-century structure that included a statue of Neptune. Platia Venizelou is packed with shops and popular cafés that spill into the adjoining Platia Kalergon, beside the leafy El Greco Garden.

d2

The Morosini Fountain takes centre stage in Platia Venizelou

Iraklio City

A figure-of-eight route from the bustling heart of Iraklio through some of the city's fascinating hidden corners and absorbing sights.

DISTANCE: 2km (1.25 miles) **ALLOW:** 2 hours

START

MOROSINI FOUNTAIN (▷ 31)
d2 Central buses

❶ Walk north from the fountain down Odos 25 Avgoustou to the seafront beside the 'Dolphin' roundabout. Bear left, then cross, with great care, to the seafront side of Sofokli Venizelou.

❷ Walk left along the seafront passing above archaeological remains. Just before the Mare Café, re-cross Sofokli Venizelou to visit the Mouseio Fisikis Istorias Kritis (▷ 28–29).

❸ Walk up the east side of the museum and turn right into Odos L. Kalokairinou. Note the fine Fountain of Idomeneus, a mix of Venetian and Ottoman features, directly opposite the museum's equally fine rear facade.

❹ Turn right at the end of the street and then, at the seafront, turn left and then left again into Odos Handakos, one of Iraklio's most appealing pedestrianized streets.

❺ Follow Handakos to, once again, reach the Morosini Fountain (Krini Morosini) in Platia Venizelou.

❻ Visit Agios Markos (▷ 30), especially if there is an art exhibition in progress. Facing out from Agios Markos, turn left and you soon pass a metal clock stand. Cross the busy Dikeosinis and explore the market street of Odos 1866.

❼ At the far end of Odos 1866 is the tree-shaded Platia Kornarou, a popular café beside the Venetian Bembo Fountain and an Ottoman-era water storage building. Turn left and follow Averof Othonos to Platia Eleftherias.

❽ Walk left round the *platia*, cross Giannari and Dikeosinis, and bear left into Dedalou, Iraklio's shopping showpiece. Follow Dedalou back to the Morosini Fountain.

END

MOROSINI FOUNTAIN
d2 Central buses

Shopping

AERAKIS
Iraklio's long-established music outlet still outclasses the big music chain stores. Aerakis specializes in Cretan and other Greek music and some international material. You can also buy the classic Cretan stringed instruments *lyras* here, starting at about €200.
e3 Odos Dedalou 37
28102 25758

BIBLIOPOLEIO/NEWS STAND
Close to the Morosini Fountain is this well run newsagent with a wide range of foreign newspapers, although most are usually a day old. It also stocks a small, varied collection of books in various languages.
d2 Platia Venizelou
28102 20135

BOOKSTORE POETRY
You'll go far in Greece to find a local bookshop with volumes by T. S. Eliot and W. H. Auden translated into Greek. This fine little bookstore, directly opposite the Archaeological Museum, deals mainly in Greek language books but also has a good range of English translations of some of Greece's finest writers.
e3 Xanthoudidi 3
28102 86758

DOLPHIN JEWELLERY
A varied and quirky selection of items, which incorporate colourful stones as well as gold and silver, is on offer at this jeweller's shop located up some steps.
e3 Odos Dedalou 4
28103 46504

ELENI KASTRINOYANNI
If you've just visited the Archaeological Museum across the road, you'll be tempted into this shop that stocks reproductions of museum items as well as Cretan handwoven embroideries, rugs, linen and jewellery.
e3 Platia Eleftherias 1
28102 26186

GALERIE DEDALOU
One of the oldest shops in Iraklio, where the old-style courtesy of proprietor Costas Papadopoulos goes well with the fine display of icons, antiques, silverware, jewellery, coins and collectibles.
e3 Odos Dedalou 11
28103 46353

IRAKLIO MARKET
Iraklio's morning market in the pedestrianized Odos 1866 is provincial Greece at its best, but with a distinctively Cretan flavour. Streetside stalls are piled high with produce. There are stalls specializing in Crete's famous dried herbs and spices, along with wild mountain honey, olives and cheese. Dry goods include leather products, multicoloured rugs and fine embroidered linen.
Odos 1866 Mon, Wed, Sat 8–2, Tue, Thu, Fri, 8–2, 5–8.30

MARKETS
As well as its main market (▷ panel), Iraklio has a lively Saturday morning market by the port that deals in a huge variety of goods from food to clothing. There is also a small fresh fish market just before the entrance to the quay leading to the Venetian Fort.

ODOS DEDALOU
The pedestrianized Odos Dedalou is Iraklio's main shopping enclave and is lined with a whole range of shops, from souvenir outlets and jewellers to numerous fashion outlets, including such well-known names as Zara and Gap.
e3

PLANET INTERNATIONAL
An international bookshop that specializes in travel guidebooks and publications in both Greek and other languages.
d2 Corner of Hortatson and Kidonias 28102 89605

TALOS PLAZA
This big shopping plaza opened in recent years. It has a huge range of shops covering most modern consumer needs. There are cafés and food outlets and an eight-screen cinema.
b1 Sofokli Venizelou

Entertainment and Activities

BIG FISH

This is one of Iraklio's biggest and busiest clubs, located on the waterfront in a restored building. Expect Greek and international DJs playing a mix of dance music.
f2 1 Arch Makariou 17
28102 88011

CAFÉ VENETO

This popular eating place transforms into an even more popular evening hangout.
e2 Epimenidou Street 9 28102 27645 All day until late

CENTRAL PARK

Serving essential coffee or drinks right on the edge of the El Greco garden, this popular place draws a stylish local crowd, starts early and keeps going into the early hours.
d2 Arkoleontos 19
28103 46500 All day until late

CORNER CAFÉ

A friendly and well-run café–bar well-placed on the corner of Platia Venizelou, at the buzzing heart of things. Ideal for people-watching over coffee or drinks.
d2 Platia Venizelou
69743 27207 All day until late

KAZANTZAKIS THEATRE

The Kazantzakis open-air theatre stages music concerts, plays and dance events during Iraklio's summer festival, and also operates as an open-air cinema in summer. For information contact the Tourist Office.
d4 Jesus Bastion, near the Oasis Gardens 28102 42977 2 and 4 Bus Station A

KORAIS

This large, brash, all-day complex has huge sports TV screens and even stages boxing matches on its spacious patio. At night there are full-on dance sessions and live performances by modern Greek bands, all to a background of decibel overkill. Great fun for funsters, all the same.
e3 Platia Korai 3
28103 46336

IRAKLIO STYLE

Nightlife in Iraklio is more sophisticated and restrained than you might find in the more up-front tourist resorts such as Malia (▷ 99). Cafés, bars and clubs are well patronized by young city Greeks who know how to have a good time, but who do not tend to binge on anything or to become aggressive. This makes the city a generally safe place to hang out in late at night. No city is perfect, however, and visitors should always take care of their belongings at all times and be aware of often fast traffic on busy roads.

ODEON CINEMA (TALOS PLAZA)

Iraklio's biggest cinema venue is located at the Talos Plaza shopping mall. It boasts eight screens showing a range of films, many being English language editions with Greek subtitles.
d2 Sofokli Venizelou
80111 60000

PAGOPOEION

Pitching to be Iraklio's classiest, funkiest and most creative venue, the transformed old city ice works realy does pull out the stops on decor (even the loos have Turner Prize potential). Jazz music features strongly here, as well as performance art and cutting-edge theatre.
e2 Platia Agios Titou
28103 46028

UTOPIA

This attractive, quirky café is in the pedestrianized Handakos, an increasingly popular street. Utopia has attractive decor and furnishings, and is a great place for good conversation and relaxing music.
d2 Handakos 51
28103 41321 All day until late

VOGUE

Another of the city's popular clubbing venues, with a fairly stylish dress code and Greek and international DJs.
d1 Sofokli Venizelou
28103 41847

Restaurants

PRICES

Prices are approximate, based on a 3-course meal for one person.

€€€ over €25
€€ €15–€25
€ under €15

BRILLANT/HERB'S GARDEN (€€–€€€)
The very stylish Brillant, on the ground floor of the Lato boutique hotel (▷ 112), operates during the winter months. The open-air Herb's Garden operates in summer on the hotel rooftop balcony with stunning views. Chef Petros Kosmadakis creates marvellous dishes, including such treats as *skioufichta*, a home-made pasta with lobster. Desserts are a joy and the wine list matches the food for quality.
e2 15 Epimenidou Street 28103 34959 Daily lunch and dinner

CAFE VENETO (€–€€)
Full of character and with friendly sevice, Veneto is on the top floor of a fine old building and has views over the harbour and the Koules Fortress. Try the Mediterranean salad with tuna, shrimps and egg.
e2 Epimenidou Street 9 28102 27645 Daily lunch and dinner

GIAKOUMIS (€)
No frills and hearty food is the style at this very traditional eatery in an alleyway off the market street of Odos 1866. Local Cretan favourites bubble happily in big cooking trays from early morning onwards.
d2 Odos Theodosaki 8 28102 84039 All day

IPPOKAMPOS (€–€€)
Undergoing complete renovation in 2010, this hugely popular local place promises to maintain its down-to-earth approach to great fish dishes, without emptying your pockets. Try for early evening as it fills up later with eager locals.
d1 Sofokli Venizelou 2810 280240 Daily lunch and dinner

PAGOPOEION (€€–€€€)
The food at this stylish place includes such treats as *velouté* of pumpkin soup with Gorgonzola, ravioli stuffed with crawfish, and salad of smoked quail breasts. Desserts are wicked, and there is a superb wine list.
e2 Platia Agios Titou 28103 46028 Daily lunch and dinner

EATING ETIQUETTE

Cretans, like all Greeks, tend to eat late in the evening. Early evening will find many Iraklio locals in the cafés around Platia Venizelou and beside the El Greco Park. After 9pm you'll find the tavernas and restaurants filling up. A service charge of about 15 per cent is usually included in the bill—certainly in towns and resorts—but you can always leave a tip if the service has been friendly and the food worthwhile.

PARASIES (€€–€€€)
This popular eatery specializes in grilled meat, but also offers some fish dishes. There's a good selection of inventive salads, incorporating local herbs and cheeses.
d2 Platia Istorikou 28102 25009 Tue–Sun lunch and dinner

PERI OREXEOS (€€)
Traditional Cretan meets modern Mediterranean at this fine little restaurant. Starters of snails with rosemary or grilled Manouri cheese, with tomatoes, introduce such signature main dishes as stir-fried pork with vegetables and white wine.
e3 Korai 10 28102 22679 Daily lunch and dinner

TOU TERZAKI (€€)
This longstanding family taverna has had a facelift. A classic dish is artichokes stuffed with cheese, while fish dishes are a feature, with such treats as *sardela sharas* (grilled sardines). Good meat and pasta dishes, too.
e2 Marineli 17 28102 21444 Daily lunch and dinner

The centre and south of this region is dominated by rugged coastline and the awesome White Mountains, while the vibrant north has the cities of Rethymno and Chania and a string of lively resorts.

Top 25

1
2
3
4
5
6
7
B
C
D
Akr Spatha
Akr Skala
Rodopou
Nisi Agria Gramvousa
Akr Vouxa
Nisi Imeri Gramvousa
749m
Onihas
Pondikonisi
762m
Geroskinos
Kolpos Kissamos
Rodopos
Kolimbari
Kolpos Hanion
Nisi Ag Theodori
Akr Mavromouri
Stavros
Chorafakia
Kambani
Korakies
Falassarna
Maleme
Damarochori
Platanias
Chania
Kissamos
Drapanias
Loutraki
Stalos
O Livadia
Episkopi
Perivolia
Souda
Platanos
Potamida
Zounaki
Mournies
Nerokouros
Limani
Pervolakia
Voukolies
Lousakies
Polirrinia
Alikianos
Kalathenes
Deres
Fournes
Gerolaki
O Kokkina Gremna
Zimbragos
848m
Skines
Kambi
Sfinari
Sineniana
Kakopetros
Plataniani
Langos
Meskla
Drakona
Kambos
Melissia
Theriso
Tiflos
Sasalos
Pal Roumata
1238m
Akr Koutoulos
Rogdia
Lakki
Kares
Livadia
Floria
Hosti
Xerakokefala
Elos
Spina
Plokamiana
Aligi
Omalos
Tzitzife
Ag Irini
O Stomiou
Moustakos
Arhondiko
Kandanos
Lefka Ori
Ethnikos Drymos Samarias
Sarakina
Agriles
2117m
2454m
Kondokinigi
Vlithias
Volakias
Pahnes
Elafonisi
Kamaria
Faragi Samarias
Ag Theodori
Prodromi
Koustogerako
O Vroulias
Spaniakos
Anidri
Sougia
Agio Roumeli
Ag Ioannis
O Selino Kastelli
Palaiochora
O Ag Roumeli
Loutro
Akr Mouros

0
20 km
0
10 miles
Akr Maleka
Akrotiri
Hordaki
Mouzouras
Sternes
Souda Bay
Allied War Cemetery
Akr Drapano
Aptera
Kalives
Kokkino Horio
Armeni
Plaka
Drapano
Vamos
Neo
Horio
Kefalas
Ormos
Almirou
Vryses
Likotinaria
Exopoli
Fres
Georgioupoli
Rethymno
Platanias
Skaleta
Pigi
Viranepiskopi
Vafes
Dramia
Gerani
Vatoudiaris
Mathes
Prines
Kirianna
Roupes
Episkopi
Somatas
Prasies
1968m
Kournas
Halara
Ag Andreas
Armeni
Kavousi
Moni
Arkadiou
Roustika
Ammoudari
Argiroupoli
Fotinos
Voleones
Asi Gonia
Geni
Imbros
Ano Malaki
Koumi
Miriokefala
Faragi
Imbrou
Ag Ioannis
Karines
Alones
Asfendou
Koxare
Spili
Komitades
Nomikiana
Sellia
Mariou
Mournes
Kissos
Chora
Sfakion
Plakias
Asomatos
Frangokastello
Gianniou
Drimiskos
Damnoni
Moni Preveli
Western Crete
E
F
G
H

Aptera

TOP 25

HIGHLIGHTS

- Roman cisterns
- Roman villa
- Monastery of St. John
- Peace and quiet

TIP

- Make sure to visit Chania's Archaeological Museum (▷ 53), where Aptera is placed in context by displays of its fascinating artefacts.

Aptera, standing on its high and windy hill above Souda Bay, is where you ring the changes through a fascinating sequence of archaeological remains that span over 3,000 years of history, all within strolling distance.

Compelling mix Aptera contains Dorian, Classical and Hellenistic Greek and Roman remains together with a Venetian monastic settlement, an Ottoman period fortress and a remnant of World War II—a compelling mix of Cretan history. During the final centuries, Aptera was a sizeable city, but much stonework was plundered in later centuries. As you approach from the village of Metohi you first come to the excavated west gate of the complex. The road continues uphill to reach a junction where the

Clockwise from top left: The isolated Turkish fortress from the Ottoman period; one of several huge Roman cisterns among the Monastic ruins; inside a three-part Roman cistern; the Monastery of St. John the Theologian

right fork leads to the main site, the left fork to the Ottoman fortress.

Lonely ruins At the main site, just north of the parking area, you will find the Monastery of St. John the Theologian, within a peaceful courtyard. To the west are huge Roman cisterns, cavernous vaults where the flap of pigeons' wings echo in the gloom. Nearby are the remains of Roman baths, and other buildings. Right by the parking area a gate allows access into olive groves, and within 100m (328ft) you come across a small Roman villa where pillars, tumbled by an earthquake, lie in chaos. Near by are the remains of a fine Roman theatre. Several metres along the track that runs towards the west gate is a World War II German machine-gun post built from ancient stonework.

THE BASICS

E3
12km (7.5 miles) east of Chania
Tue–Sun 8.30–3
Only accessible by car
None
Free
The Ottoman fortress is currently (2011) being renovated and access is not assured until further notice

Chania

TOP 25

HIGHLIGHTS

- The Venetiko Limani (Venetian harbour)
- Archaeological Museum (▷ 53)
- Byzantine Museum (▷ 54)
- Old quarter

TIP

- Seek out the tiny Jewish synagogue with its lovely courtyard off Odos Kondilaki, and the little Folklore Museum in the courtyard of the Roman Catholic church off Odos Halidon.

In Chania you can dream of wooden sailing ships and the rattle and hum of a medieval Venetian world as you stroll alongside the lapping waters of the ancient harbour and through the labyrinthine alleyways of the old town.

Ancient city Chania, the ancient city of Kydonia, is the modern 'capital' of Western Crete. It became a focus of Cretan life on the decline of Knossos. But Chania, too, fell into decline during the Arab occupation of the ninth and 10th centuries, only to rise once more during the Venetian period (1204–1645) as La Canea, 'the Venice of the East'. The city fell under Ottoman control from 1645 to 1898 and survived as the island's capital until 1971. Such an exotic history has left the old town and

Clockwise from far left: Bougainvillea decorates a small alleyway in the Spiantza quarter; a minaret towers over the appealing narrow streets; restaurants, cafés and hotels line the harbour front; the harbour at sunset; the Mosque of the Jannisaries

harbour area of Chania with irresistible antique appeal, although the modern city surrounds it all with a brash and thoroughly Greek vibrancy.

Ideal base The city is an ideal base for exploring western Crete but it is also a superb tourist destination in its own right. The waterfront area of the inner harbour encompasses the old domed Mosque of the Janissaries and the Venetian arsenals. Behind the eastern section of the famously picturesque outer harbour is a satisfying maze of tangled alleyways where Venetian and Ottoman houses have been restored with style. Round every corner are elegant balconies and doorcases, and the narrow streets are punctuated by quirky shops and galleries, some of the best restaurants in Crete and hidden corners of enduring appeal.

THE BASICS

D2

Numerous cafés, tavernas and restaurants, especially at the harbour

Regular services to and from outlying areas and to Rethymno and Iraklio

M. Mylonogianni, tel 28210 36155

Elafonisi

TOP 25

Perfect isolation (left); a narrow strip of water between Elafonisi and the mainland (right)

THE BASICS

- B4
- 40km (25 miles) south of Kissamos
- A few cafés and tavernas nearby
- Twice a day from Chania and Rethymno
- Ferries from Palaiochora
- None, but some of the wooden walkways may be accessible to sturdy wheelchairs

HIGHLIGHTS

- Wading to the off-shore island
- Spotting wild birds
- Swimming in the crystal-clear water
- Learning about wild flowers

The semi-tropical beach of Elafonisi reaches out towards Africa and shares a sense of the latter's exoticism. Perfect beaching and fantastic wildlife make Elafonisi a paradise regained.

Valued wildlife Elafonisi's designation as a National Park has enhanced its already fabulous nature. In high summer the ambience fades a touch, as busloads of fellow visitors arrive from Chania (▷ 42–43) and boatloads from Palaiochora (▷ 52). Increased human pressure means some control on access; areas of vegetation and geologically important sites are fenced off. All visitors are asked to respect these laudable restrictions. There's still plenty left for family-friendly fun on the lovely sand and pebble beaches that slide gently into tiny lagoons of turquoise water.

Beautiful shoreline Elafonisi supports more than one hundred bird species, and resident birds include kestrel, white wagtail and the Sardinian warbler, while migrating birds include purple heron, hoopoe and skylark. The area also supports such vulnerable plant species as sea holly, sea spurge, the endangered sea daffodil and the winter flowering *androcymbium rechingeri*. Useful information boards describe the plant life. As if this richness of wildlife plus the shoreline beaches were not enough, you can wade out across a natural causeway of sand to the island off Elafonisi and explore its equally splendid natural beauty.

View over the gorge (left); donkey trail (middle); narrow part of the rock walls (right)

Faragi Imbrou

The iconic Samaria Gorge may be at the top of your tick list, but Crete is zipped apart by many other dramatic gorges that make for fantastic alternatives to the Samaria's sometimes heel-to-toe samba.

Rewarding walking The Faragi Imbrou (Imbros Gorge) is a small-scale version of Samaria (▷ 46), but it packs the same punch. It is growing in popularity and part of the E4 long-distance path runs through it, but the trip is still far more peaceful than Samaria at its busiest. This was part of the traditional donkey route across the hard lands of Sfakia, and sections of the old cobbled trail *(kalderimi)* survive. After the Battle of Crete Allied soldiers retreated through the gorge to Chora Sfakion (▷ 54) from where about three-quarters of them were evacuated by the Royal Navy; the rest were taken prisoner and marched back through the gorge to Chania.

Soaring walls The gorge is about 8km (5 miles) long, and you should allow from 2 to 3 hours for the trip. For added effort and time you can walk uphill from the village of Komitades on the coast, east of Chora Sfakion. Better to freewheel down, however, from a starting point south of Imbros village. The gorge has all the ingredients of its bigger rivals with green, open sections vying with narrow defiles between soaring rock walls. From the walk's end at Komitades it's a hot 5km (3-mile) walk by road to Chora Sfakion, or you can call a taxi.

THE BASICS

- E4
- 54km (33 miles) southeast of Chania
- May–Oct (depending on weather) 7am–sunset
- Cafés and tavernas in Imbros and Komitades
- Three a day from Chania and Chora Sfakion
- Not suitable
- Wear sturdy footwear and take plenty to drink

HIGHLIGHTS

- Wild flowers in spring
- Spectacular rock architecture
- Peace and quiet early in the season

TIP

- Do not be tempted into the gorge in winter. Heavy rains and snowmelt can trigger flash floods into an already swollen stream.

Faragi Samarias

TOP 25

HIGHLIGHTS

- The Iron Gates
- Spotting a lammergeier (bearded vulture), if lucky
- Wild flowers in spring and early summer
- Reaching the sea

TIP

- If you are looking for a great hike, head up the rocky path to the top of Mount Gingilos (13km/8 miles). Sturdy boots and mountain walking and rock scrambling experience are essential.

This is Crete's big beast of a gorge: 16km (10 miles) of rough rambling through a fabulous rift in the Lefka Ori. You may be nose-to-tail with other hikers in high season, but it's a great trip all the same.

Deep descent The Faragi Samarias (Samaria Gorge) accommodates anything up to 2,000 people a day in high season, so compelling is this awesome place. The gorge plunges steeply from its starting point beneath the gaunt face of Mount Gingilos at the edge of the Omalos Plain into the deep heart of the Lefka Ori. The initial descent is down the *xiloskalon,* a mix of rock steps and wooden stairways that twist and turn steeply to the bed of the gorge. From here you keep going alongside a stream bed through always dramatic scenery. About halfway is the

Clockwise from left: Steps down to the start of the Samaria Gorge walk; a stream trickling through the Samaria Valley; Mount Gingilos at the northern end of the gorge; wild flowers thrive on the mountainside in spring and summer

village of Samaria itself, abandoned in the early 1960s when the gorge and its environs were designated as a National Park.

Narrow walls Beyond the old village the way crosses and recrosses the stream between ever-narrowing walls until it reaches the famous Iron Gates, where the rock walls soar 305m (1,000ft) on either side and are a bare 2m (6ft) apart. Soon the walls relent and you head on through the near-deserted old village of Agia Roumeli, to reach its beachside counterpart where iced drinks and a soothing sea await. The Samaria walk can take anything up to seven hours and although the sheer pressure of people reduces the chance of spotting wildlife, there are Cretan wild goats (*agrimi*, nick-named *kri-kri*) in the area. You might be lucky.

THE BASICS

D4

43km (27 miles) south of Chania

28210 67140; head of gorge 28210 67179

May–Oct (depends on weather) 7am–3pm. From 3pm until sunset visitors are permitted only to walk 2km (1.5 miles) into the gorge, from either end

Tavernas at the head of the gorge and at Agia Roumeli; take refreshments for the gorge

Moni Arkadiou

TOP 25

Church of Moni Arkadiou (left); former gun powder magazine (right)

THE BASICS

- H4
- 24km (15 miles) southeast of Rethymno
- 28310 83126
- Daily 9–7
- Café–taverna opposite
- Three a day Mon–Fri from Rethymno
- Access to monastery only
- Inexpensive

HIGHLIGHTS

- The facade of the monastery church
- The powder magazine
- Garden courtyard

TIP

- For a powerful fictionalized account of the events of 1866 read the novel *Freedom and Death* by Nikos Kazantzakis.

Dark deeds were done at this most iconic of Cretan monasteries; but don't expect to be downcast. There is an absorbing sense of dramatic history here, and of the irrepressible Cretan spirit of resistance.

Splendid isolation Moni Arkadiou has always held the high ground of Cretan history. Its isolated position, high in the Ideon Mountains, made it a focus of resistance against Crete's multifarious invaders and occupiers. Disasters happened however, and today the monastery holds iconic status as a symbol of martyrdom and Cretan heroism against Ottoman rule. The monastery's church boasts an outstanding Baroque facade, crowned by a triple bell tower. The church is at the centre of a walled compound lined with cloisters and buildings, and dotted with greenery.

Bold rebellion No other aspect of that past is quite so revered as the events of 9 November 1866, during a rebellion against Ottoman rule when hundreds of Cretan fighters and their families took refuge in the monastery. They were besieged for two days before the western gate was breached. As the Muslim troops poured into the compound, the vaulted powder magazine blew up with savage effect, killing hundreds of Cretan men, women and children and many of the attackers. The enduring story is that the Cretans fired the magazine deliberately rather than succumb. You can see the roofless powder magazine in the monastery grounds.

Monks' quarters (left); Church of St. John (middle); view over Moni Preveli (right)

Moni Preveli

Let your spirits soar at Moni Preveli, not only because of the monastery's lovely coastal spot but because of the thrilling part it played in saving many allied soldiers during World War II.

Noble survivor The Moni Prevali of today dates from the 17th century, when the hard-pressed monks chose to abandon their original home as Crete fell to the Ottoman Empire. The atmospheric remains of this older monastery, Kato Moni Preveli, stand by the roadside about 3km (2 miles) before you reach the present monastery. Moni Preveli stands high above the sea and has a magical atmosphere. It was rebuilt in 1835, and was then partially destroyed by German forces in the 1940s as reprisal for the crucial part played by the monks in helping Allied soldiers to escape the island after the Battle of Crete.

Breathtaking views The finest feature is the Church of Agios Ioannis (St. John), which is a 19th-century reconstruction of the original 17th-century church. It contains a crucifix said to be a fragment of the True Cross. In the monastery's courtyard is a beautiful fountain overlooked by a palm tree on the upper terrace. The view south from the monastery to the Paximadhia Islands is breathtaking. A museum is to the left of the main entrance, and beyond are several memorial plaques celebrating the courageous part played by the monks in helping Allied troops to escape after the Battle of Crete in 1941.

THE BASICS

www.preveli.org

G5

13km (8 miles) east of Plakias

28320 31246

Apr, May daily 8.30–7; Jun–Oct Mon–Sat 8.30–1.30, 3.30–7

Snack bar summer only (€)

Four a day from Rethymno

Excellent

Inexpensive

HIGHLIGHTS

- Church of Agios Ioannis
- Venetian fountain
- The museum
- Memorial plaques

TIP

- Make sure to make a stop just before reaching the monastery at a garden memorial celebrating the monks assistance to Allied soldiers. The garden features larger than life bronze statues of an Allied soldier and a Greek Orthodox abbot, both wielding rifles.

Rethymno

TOP 25

HIGHLIGHTS

- Archaeological Museum (▷ 56)
- The Fortezza
- Old town
- Promenade and beach

TIP

- Try to catch a musical performance at the Temenos Nerantze (Neratzies Mosque). Enquire at the Mosque's office for details (▷ 65).

Rethymno flies a friendly flag for Cretan culture and is home to the University of Crete. There's still the easygoing life, however, with outstanding restaurants, cafés and bars, and one of the best town beaches on the island.

Cultural centre During the 16th century the Venetians built one of their huge fortresses at Rethymno and established the town as a trading centre. On the fall of Constantinople, when many Byzantine scholars came to Crete, Rethymno became a major intellectual and cultural centre of the post-medieval world. The Ottomans controlled the city from 1645 until the beginning of the 20th century and today their architectural influence survives in such superb buildings as the Neratzies Mosque. The

Clockwise from top left: Narrow alleys are characteristic of the old quarter; the pristine, white facade of Rethymno church; detail of the Neratzies Mosque; looking along the beach towards the old town; restaurants and bars illuminate the inner harbour at dusk; inside one of Rethymno's many fine restaurants

old quarter of Rethymno is full of Venetian and Ottoman architectural features, and round every corner you come across handsome stone doorcases and ornate wooden balconies.

Great shopping The narrow, pedestrianized alleys of the old town are a pleasure to stroll through (▷ 61) and are dotted with fine restaurants and little shops selling everything from classy artworks to leather goods, jewellery, herbs, spices and raki. The town is dominated by the massive Venetian fortress (▷ 56) on a high and rocky headland. South of the fortress is the attractive Venetian harbour from where the town beach runs alongside a long water-front with walkways and palm trees. West of the harbour is the heart of the old town, around the Venetian Rimondi Fountain.

THE BASICS

- G3
- Numerous
- Regular services to and from outlying areas and to and from Chania and Iraklio
- Delfini Building, Eleftheriou Venizelou; tel 28310 29148

Palaiochora

TOP 25

A view across to the eastern beach (left); the sheltered western beach (right)

THE BASICS

C4

80km (50 miles) southwest of Chania

Numerous tavernas

Five a day Mon–Sat from Chania

In summer, ferries to Sougia, Agia Roumeli, Loutro, Chora Sfakion and the island of Gavdos (Gavdos limited in winter)

Few

Pebble Beach seafront; tel 28230 41507

HIGHLIGHTS

- Sandy beach
- Boat trips
- Taking it easy

At Palaiochora the beaches lie to either side of a narrow peninsula, which juts out from Crete's rugged south coast as if determined to chase the sun as far as it can towards Africa.

Friendly spirit A one-time fishing hamlet, Palaiochora has managed to preserve a spirit of friendliness and ease despite being a still expanding and unquestionable 'resort'. There's a quirky sense of disorientation for first time visitors between the peninsula's east side, Pebble Beach, with its rugged boulder-strewn shore and its west side and star turn, Sandy Beach where sun, sand and sea rule—although it's breezy enough at times to provide good windsurfing. Between the two, the village's cheerful main street dispenses tributary streets to either side that trickle down to the shining sea.

Scenic coast At the southern tip of the peninsula are the ruins of Selinou, a 13th-century Venetian castle that overlooks Palaiochora's harbour and marina. The mountainous coast runs all the way to Elafonisi (▷ 44) in the west and Sougia (▷ 58) in the east. West from Palaiochora, a dreary coastal road weaves between plastic greenhouses where tomatoes are grown. The road ends at the pebbly Krios (Cold) beach, so named because of fresh-water springs that chill the sea. Beyond here, the coastal E4 path is worth following either to small beaches (often clothes optional) or all the way to Elafonisi through challenging cliffside sections.

More to See

ARGIROUPOLI

At Argiroupoli, in the foothills of the White Mountains, spring water tumbles down wooded slopes to the lower village where it is harnessed by a clutch of roadside tavernas into trout ponds and ornamental watermills. High above is the upper village, where the church has a handsome Venetian portal and belltower. Next to the church are some excavated remnants of the Greek-Roman town of Lappa.

F4 25km (16 miles) southwest of Rethymno Tavernas and cafés Three a day Mon–Fri from Rethymno Few

CHANIA: ARCHAIOLOGIKO MOUSEIO

This fine collection in the vaulted Venetian Church of St. Francis, spans the period from late Neolithic (1500BC) through the Minoan and Mycenaean era to the Roman occupation. Some splendid Roman mosaics take centre stage, and a large glass case crammed with clay bulls, used as sacred offerings, substitutes for the real thing. Look for the cheerful little statue of Hercules. A side annexe has an exhibition of superb pieces from the Mitsotakis collection, and an adjoining garden has a preserved well from the Ottoman period.

D2 Odos Halidon 21 28210 90334 Tue–Sun 8.30–3 Cafés and tavernas in Odos Halidon or on the harbour Good Moderate; combined ticket available with Byzantine Museum (▷ 54)

CHANIA: NAFTIKO MOUSEIO

Exhibits at this Naval Museum are an earnest celebration of Crete's sea trade and naval warfare, and range from models of Bronze Age boats to late 20th-century submarines. The collection also contains marine weapons and instruments, historical documents and an exhibition about the 1941 Battle of Crete.

D2 Fort Firkas, Akti Kountourioti 28210 91875 Daily 8.30–2; closed public hols Harbour restaurants None Moderate

The picturesque village of Argiroupoli

The tranquil garden outside the Archaiologiko Mouseio in Chania

CHANIA: VIZANTINO MOUSEIO

This peaceful little Byzantine Museum is housed in the old Venetian Church of St. Salvatore, (converted into a mosque during the Ottoman period), beneath Chania's old fortress walls. Exhibits include early Christian sculptures and engravings, a fine mosaic fragment, Byzantine wall paintings and icons and Venetian sculpture.

D2 Odos Theotokopoulou 82 28210 96046 Tue–Sun 8–3 Cafés and tavernas on the harbour Very good Inexpensive; combined ticket available with Archaeological Museum (▷ 53)

CHORA SFAKION

During the 16th century Chora Sfakion was the largest town on the south coast with a population of 3,000, but the Sfakia area as a whole suffered appallingly for its spirited resistance to the Ottoman occupation. Much of Chora was destroyed, and what was left was more or less flattened by German bombers during World War II. Today Chora Sfakion is a small resort with a pebbly beach and ferry quay. It is very busy in high season as a bus-ferry transit for walkers going to and from the Samaria Gorge

E4 67km (42 miles) south of Chania Seafront tavernas Three a day to Chania; one a day to Plakias Ferries to Agia Roumeli (Samaria Gorge), Loutro, Sougia, Palaiochora and the island of Gavdos

FALASSARNA

Increasing swathes of 'plasticultura' (plastic greenhouse development) have advanced on the one-time unspoilt beach of Falassarna. This is still a prime venue for beach lovers, all the same. A fascinating bonus lies north of the beach at the scattered remnants of a Hellenistic city-state with tombs, quarries, towers, water cisterns and the ruins of houses and storerooms. A high point is the row of terracotta 'hip baths' that lie beneath a protective corrugated iron canopy.

Chora Sfakion when the sun goes down

B2 8km (5 miles) northwest of Platanos Tavernas above the beach Three a day from Kissamos None

FRANGOKASTELLO

This great castle, which is built of ruby-red stone, stands like a film-set fortress beside the sea. Now an empty shell, it was built by the Venetians in 1340. In 1770 the Sfakiot rebel leader, Daskaloyiannis, was forced to surrender to the Turks here, and in 1828, during the Greek War of Independence, the Greek leader, Hadzi Michali Daliani, along with several hundred Cretans, died defending the fort against the Turks. You can doze in the sun on the beautiful beach below and dream of the phantom warriors of Daliani, the Dew Shadows, who are said to march round the castle at dawn.

E5 17km (11 miles) east of Chora Sfakion Several tavernas One a day from Rethymno via Chora Sfakion; one a day from Plakias None Free

GEORGIOUPOLI

A cheerful mix of still viable fishing village and dedicated tourist resort, Georgioupoli lies on the south side of the River Almiros. It has a long sandy beach that is ideal for families, although rough seas, when strong offshore currents are made worse, should be avoided. Inland the town is a charming jumble of villas, pensions, rooms, tavernas and shops centred round a bustling central square.

F3 22km (14 miles) west of Rethymno Tavernas and cafés on the main square Hourly service to Rethymno and Chania Few

LOUTRO

Car-free and easygoing Loutro is a refreshing place to escape to—the only access is on foot or by boat. The village's scribble of white and blue houses lies between the mighty Lefka Ori Mountains and the Libyan Sea; idyllic enough, although boat-borne visitors swell the numbers by day. There are several

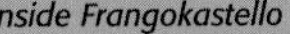

Inside Frangokastello

Loutro stands on a crescent bay

taverns and cafés and a handful of places to stay. The small pebble beach will do, and you can always hop on a boat or hire a canoe to reach the sands of Marmara and Sweetwater Beach.

E4 5km (3 miles) west of Chora Sfakion The Blue House (▷ 66) Ferry to Chora Sfakion and Agia Roumeli None

PLAKIAS

The splendid location of Plakias, on a coastal plain between rugged mountains and a long swathe of sand and shingle beach, has seen a rapid expansion of this popular resort. A spacious seafront adds to its sunny openness—even the little harbour wall is decorated by colourful motifs. There are better beaches at nearby Damnoni, which can be reached by car or by a pleasant 30-minute walk.

F4 35km (22 miles) south of Rethymno Cafés and tavernas Seven a day from Rethymno Few

RETHYMNO: ARCHAIOLOGIKO MOUSEIO

Housed in the rather grim monolithic building that was, unsurprisingly, the former prison during the Ottoman period, this well-organized museum has a fine collection of Minoan and Graeco-Roman finds from the Rethymno region. Highlights include little clay figurines of bulls and people, a serpentine lamp and a boar's tusk helmet, all from the Minoan period. Graeco-Roman artefacts include exquisite bronze pots and figurines, a vase depicting a rather rude satyr, and a fragment of an inscribed stone recording a 600-450BC law against binge drinking.

G3 Odos Himaras 28310 54668 Tue–Sun 8.30–3 Cafés on the nearby seafront None Moderate

RETHYMNO: FORTEZZA

Fabulous views are a major feature of Rethymno's late 16th-century fortress, said to be the largest Venetian fort ever built. It failed

Detail of a sarcophogus in the Archaiologiko Mouseio, Rethymno

dismally in its purpose, however, as the invading Ottoman troops of 1645 simply ignored it, took the city and starved out the Fortezza's garrison in three weeks. Later, earthquakes and German bombs damaged the structure and today restoration continues. A main feature inside is a restored mosque built for the Turkish garrison.

G3 Odos Katehaki 28310 28101 Apr–Oct daily 8.30–7.30; Nov–Mar 8.30–6 Snack bar (€) None Moderate

RETHYMNO: ISTORIKO KAI LAOGRAFIKO MOUSEIO

In a restored Venetian house with a garden, near the Neratzies Mosque (▷ 65), this Folk Museum houses a charming collection of crafts from local homes, including fine samples of embroidery, lace, basketware, pottery, knives and agricultural tools. Labelling in English accompanies displays of bread-making methods, Greek needlework and other traditional rural crafts.

G3 M. Vernadou 28 28310 23398 Mon–Sat 9.30–2, 6–8 (winter openings are not fixed) Cafés and taverns nearby Few Moderate

RETHYMNO: KENTRO SIGKRONIS EKASTIKIS DIMIORGEAS

The stylish whitewashed interiors of this excellent modern Municipal Art Gallery display changing exhibitions of often challenging and provocative contemporary painting, sculpture and other media, mainly by Greek artists. It also has a permanent collection of Greek art (only part of which is on view at any one time).

G3 Odos Himaras 28310 55847 Apr–Oct Tue–Fri 9–1, 7–10, Sun 11–3; Nov–Mar Tue–Fri 10–2, 6–9, Sat–Sun 11–3 In old town None Moderate

SOUDA BAY ALLIED WAR CEMETERY

The compelling and deeply moving World War II cemetery on the shores of Souda Bay is

Walls of the Venetian fortress, Rethymno

unquestionably the best tended acre in all of Crete. Row after row of symmetrical white headstones, their bases stained red from the Cretan earth, stand to attention among cropped green grass. The graves are of 1,497 Allied soldiers who died defending Crete in World War II. The names of the many soldiers are listed in the cemetery register, which is kept in a box at the entrance to the building.

✚ E3 ✉ 5km (3 miles) southeast of Chania harbour ☎ None ⏲ All day every day 🍴 Tavernas and cafés in Souda 🚌 Hourly service from Chania to Souda Bay and then a short walk ♿ Good; phone ahead of visit

SOUGIA

It's a long, long way to Sougia—but it's worth it. Tucked below the mighty Lefka Ori mountains, this one time handful of fishing shacks behind a long pebble beach has grown into a beach resort, which is still human in scale and is happily ragged round the edges. To the west of the village, reached by a local boat or by a splendid gorge and plateau walk, lie the haunting Greek and Roman ruins of the ancient city of Lissos. Part of a Roman mosaic is the outstanding feature.

✚ C4 ✉ 70km (43 miles) southwest of Chania 🍴 Tavernas in the resort 🚌 Three a day from Chania ⛴ May–Sep daily ferries to Agia Roumeli, Chora Sfakion and Palaiochora ♿ None

VRYSES

Everyday life and traditional charm wrap themselves round Vryses, where the traffic-logged main street bids fit to rival downtown Iraklio. Visit in winter and early spring and the gushing river and its foaming weir may remind you of northern European mountain villages. Things dry up in summer, but there's still plenty of charm in this Cretan country town.

✚ E3 ✉ 46km (28 miles) southeast of Chania 🍴 Tavernas in the resort 🚌 Three a day from Rethymno and Chania

Looking down over a tiny clifftop church to Sougia Bay

Chania City

Stroll round Chania's inner harbour, then inland through the old town and back to the Venetiko Limani (Venetian harbour).

DISTANCE: 3km (1.8 miles) **ALLOW:** 2 hours, including sightseeing

START

MOSQUE OF THE JANISSARIES (▷ 42–43) D2

❶ Walk northeast along the harbourside Akti Tombazi, with the restored Venetian arsenals on your right. These old arsenals are now the Centre for Mediterranean Architecture.

❷ Turn right into the cobbled Platia Georgiou Katehaki. Cross the *platia* to its left inner corner and then turn left. After a few metres turn right into Odos A. Choleontos.

❸ Go right again into Odos Kanevaro, an area known as Kastelli, the historical site of Kidonia, ancient Chania. Midway along the street, below street level, is a covered area of ancient ruins.

❹ Continue downhill to reach Platia El Venizelou, just inland from the old harbour. Cross diagonally left and then turn right into Zambeliou. Zambeliou leads into the heart of the old town.

❺ Just before an archway, turn right into Theotokopoulou Portou.

❻ Follow this road to its end and to the seafront. Just before Theotokopoulou Portou descends gently to the seafront, at a breach in the old city walls, is the Byzantine Museum (▷ 54) on your right.

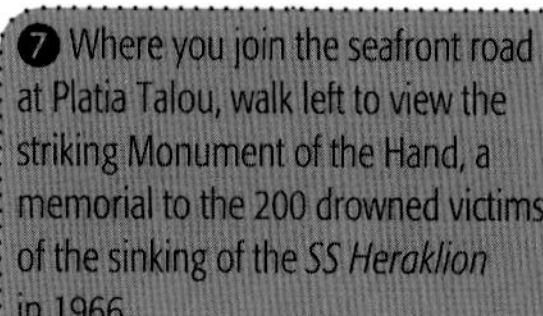

❼ Where you join the seafront road at Platia Talou, walk left to view the striking Monument of the Hand, a memorial to the 200 drowned victims of the sinking of the *SS Heraklion* in 1966.

❽ Walk back to the north and follow the seafront road to reach the outer harbour.

VENETIAN HARBOUR D2

END

Rethymno

A quiet, circular walk round Rethymno from the seafront, visiting the Venetian Fortezza, old town and the city's cathedral.

DISTANCE: 2km (1.5 miles) **ALLOW:** 2 hours

START

VENETIAN HARBOUR (▷ 50–51)
G3

END

ELEFTHERIOU VENIZELOU
G3

1. Walk north round the Venetian Harbour. At the final café, Café Nuvel (▷ 66), cross the road and turn right. Continue past Hotel Ideon (▷ 110) and a line of cafés and tavernas.

2. By the last roadside taverna go up the steps past the Thalassografia Café to reach a paved road that leads between the Archaeological Museum (▷ 56) and the Fortezza (▷ 56).

3. Continue down the side of the museum and turn left down Himaras, passing the Municipal Art Gallery (▷ 57) near the bottom.

4. At a T-junction, turn right and then left in a few yards to Xanthoudou and into the heart of the old town.

5. Go straight across a junction, and at the next junction with Vernadou turn left and pass the Neratzies Mosque (▷ 65); you may hear classical music wafting from within the building.

6. Just past the mosque turn right and follow Ethnikis Andistaseos to its end, just before the Porta Guora, the old city gate.

7. Just before the gate and by an old well in the middle of the little square, turn left down Tombazi to reach Cathedral Square.

8. Beyond the cathedral turn left, then bear right and go left along Arkadiou to reach the 17th-century Venetian loggia, where a right turn leads to Eleftheriou Venizelou.

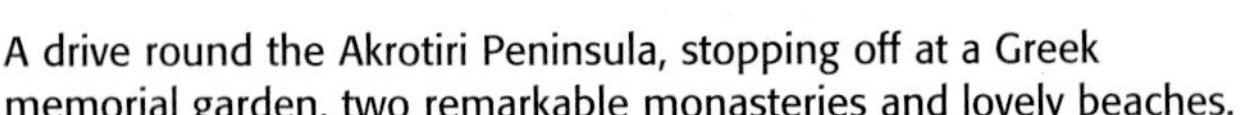

Akrotiri Peninsula

A drive round the Akrotiri Peninsula, stopping off at a Greek memorial garden, two remarkable monasteries and lovely beaches.

DISTANCE: 45km (28 miles) **ALLOW:** 6 hours, including stops

START

CHANIA (▷ 42–43)
D2

❶ Leave Chania going east and follow signs for the airport. At the top of a long uphill section, at a broad junction, turn left and follow signs for the Venizelos Graves.

❷ In 2km (1.25 miles), by a supermarket on your right, turn left at an awkward junction and then go left again.

❸ In about 50m (54 yards) turn left to a parking area. The graves lie in a peaceful garden with stunning views over Chania.

❹ Return to the main road and go left, and left again at a roundabout signed airport. Follow signs for Agia Triada and Moni Gouvernetou. Make a right signed Moni Gouvernetou to reach Moni Agia Triada.

❺ Leave the monastery, turn right through beautiful hills to the 16th-century Gouvernetou Monastery.

❻ From the monastery a path, steep in places (2.5 hours there and back), descends to a beautiful gorge past the atmospheric Cave of St. John the Hermit to the dramatic ruins of Katholiko Monastery.

❼ Return to Agia Triada and turn right along the tree-lined avenue. At the junction go right, signposted Chorafakia. Keep straight on at the next junction, and again at the next signed Stavros, to reach the beach resort of that name.

❽ Return to Chorafakia and keep right at the junction by a garage, signposted Chania. Stop at Kalathas Beach on the way back to Chania.

CHANIA
D2

END

ATELIER POTTERY WORKSHOP

www.frosso-bora.com
At this little workshop below the Atelier rooms (▷ 109) is the workshop of Frosso Bora, where she crafts a range of charming and reasonably priced ceramic ware.
G3 Odos Himaras 27, Rethymno 28310 24440
Apr–Oct

BOOKSTORE

A crammed little niche in the narrow Souliou, the Bookstore does just that, keeps its busy shelves full of second-hand books of all types and in all languages, although a good Greek selection keeps the flag flying.
G3 Souliou 43, Rethymno 28310 54307

BROTHERS KIMIONIS

A longstanding business, the Brothers Kimionis overflows with all kinds of spices, olive oils, honey, herbs and Cretan tea.
G3 Odos Paleologou 29–31, Rethymno 28310 55667

CARMELA

More stylish gallery than shop, this is where Carmela Iatropoulou and her husband create beautiful ceramics and paintings. There are also original works of art from all over Greece; all made using traditional techniques.
D2 Odos Angelou 7, Chania 28210 90487

EN CHORDIAS

One of Rethymno's most fascinating shops, where Manolis Katzantonis crafts exquisite traditional instruments such as the three-stringed fiddle, the *lyra,* and the double-stringed *laouto*. A must for musicians and music lovers. You may even catch an impromptu performance from passing aficionados.
G3 Kallergi 38, Rethymno 28310 29043

ERGOXEIRO

A charmingly old fashioned shop specializing in Cretan embroidery and linenwork. You can buy small pieces for a few euros, but the top-end Rethymno designs may charm several hundred not so old-fashioned euros from you.
G3 Odos Arkadiou 62, Rethymno 28310 26734

CRETAN POPULAR ART

Kentro Kritikis Laikis Texnis (Centre of Cretan Popular Art) is very different from the usual souvenir-shop experience. This recently launched co-operative venture, located in part of an old monastery, is worth a visit to see Cretan weavers, potters, sculptors, painters and even bookbinders busy in their workshops. It also has an exhibition hall, film theatre and much information on Cretan crafts, and you can buy work made on the premises.
G3 15–17 Kritovoulidou (alleyway between south ends of Arkadiou and Gerakari), Rethymno 08310 51501

IKARUS

A superb collection of Greek ceramics and other craftwork makes this fine gallery a must. Prices range from the affordable to several hundred euros, but everything is by Greek craftspeople and includes such leading lights as Costas Panaretos and Vorhos Kokovlis. Ceramic work by Irini Lakkas is especially fine.
D2 Zambeliou 52, Chania 28210 95475

LEATHER LANE

There's a nice whiff of the old Ottoman souk here as traders persuade and cajole you to buy such leather goods as bags, belts, wallets, shoes, slippers and other souvenirs.
D2 Odos Skridlof, Chania

MEDITERRANEO BOOKSTORE

This well-stocked bookshop sells foreign language newspapers and has a good selection of thrillers and a thoughtful spread of books on Greece. It's on the far side of the inner harbour, near the Naval Museum
D2 Akti Koundourioti 57, Chania 28210 86904
Mar–Oct

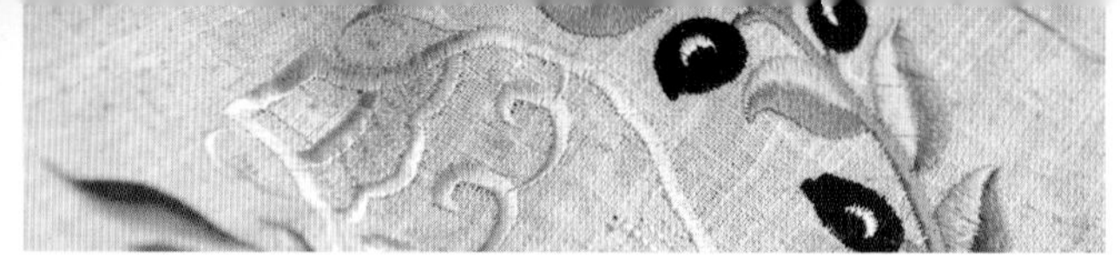

NIKOS SIRAGAS WOOD ART

The authentic and talented artist Nikos Siragas works at his lathe in his Rethymno gallery on most summer evenings. His work is functional but also creative.

G3 Petalioti 2, Rethymno 28310 23010 Apr–Oct

OMODAMOS

A typical little cave of a shop in the atmospheric Souliou, Omodamos has a colourful and quirky selection of fine ceramics from a number of distinctive Cretan potters.

G3 Souliou 3, Rethymno 28310 58763

PANTOS KAIROU

This wonderful little shop may go to your head in a big way. Here Maria Giannopoulou makes cheerful and stylish hats in a variety of materials, while Giorgios Konstadinidis crafts unique and quirky artefacts from tin. Scarves, wraps and bags add to the treasures.

D2 6 Odos Skoufon, Chania 28210 57037

PARA ORO

Check for the quirky clock built into the 'O' of Ora above the door of this little art shop that is full of intriguing and unusual ceramics, little boats and other objects crafted out of metal and glass.

D2 Odos Theotokopoulou 16, Chania 28210 88990

RETHYMNO WEEKLY MARKET

A colourful extravaganza of great food and bric-a-brac is staged in Rethymno every Thursday near the Public Gardens and the old city gate, the Porto Guora. Everything from olives, nails, fruit that tastes like fruit and Cretan herbs, plus clothing, is available.

G3 Odos Dimitrakaki and Odos Koundouriotou, Rethymno Thu 8am–1pm

SELECTED

Handbag haven of designer chic; you'll find pricey French and Italian labels such as the quirky Braccialini and the svelte Le Tanneur here, but with more reasonably priced options also.

G3 Arkadiou 153, Rethymno 28310 26996

CHANIA MARKET

Chania's covered market dates from 1913 and is on a grand scale, cruciform in shape and modelled on the Marseilles' market, with entrances at either end. Food produce is the main attraction with swathes of fruit and vegetables, herbs and honey, spices and dried fruits, oils and wine. Stallholders are born performers and the atmosphere is never less than vibrant and cheerful. Scattered throughout the market are no-frills eating places.

D2 Platia S Venizelou, Chania Mon, Wed, Thu, Sat 8–2, Tue, Fri 8.30–1.30, 9–8 (summer 6–9)

THALLO

This tiny shop specializes in *anthokosmimat*, the art of gilding flowers and leaves to make distinctive jewellery. Prices start at about €45 for gold and silver leaf necklaces on leather halters, to several hundred euros for decorative olive wreaths in gold.

G3 Arkadiou 88, Rethymno 28310 68144

TOP HANAS

There's a wonderful selection of loom-made kilims (tapestry woven carpets) and rugs in this atmospheric cave-like shop at the heart of the old town.

D2 Odos Angelou 3–5 (near the Naval Museum), Chania 28210 98571

YDRIA

A well-stocked pottery with a particularly fine line in colourful glazing—lovely blue and orange pots and dishes—Ydria has other quality artefacts for sale in this roadside shop in the tiny village of Asomatos, near Plakias.

G4 Asomatos 28320 31125

Entertainment and Activities

BOAT EXCURSIONS

The classic cruise boat *Irini* heads for the islands of Lazaretto and Agii Theodorou from Chania's outer harbour in summer.
D2 Chania Harbour 28210 52001

CINE APOLLON/ ASTERIA

Rethymno's cinemas, the indoor Apollon for winter outings and the outdoor Asteria for warm summer evenings, ring the changes with mainly English language films subtitled in Greek.

Cine Apollon
G3 Mesolongiou 18, Rethymno 28310 29520 Daily 8pm

Asteria
G3 Melissinou 23, Rethymno 28310 22830 Daily 8pm

CLUBS IN CHANIA

Although Chania has no mega-clubs, Odos Sourmeli, behind the southern harbourfront cafés, has a clutch of raucous late-night spots such as Cafebaroom, Point Bar, Scorpio and Klik, all with similar playlists, ranging from pop to Greek rock.

DIVE2GETHER

www.dive2gether.com
Based at Plakias, this reliable business organizes diving and snorkelling trips for all ages in the crystal clear waters off Crete's south coast where visibility is up to 40m (131ft). Full PADI courses are run as well as leisure dives.
F4 Plakias 28320 32313 Apr–Oct

FIGARO

This is the place to chill in relaxed company and against a background of the coolest sounds, all in the shadow of the minaret of the Neratzies Mosque.
G3 Vernardou 21, Rethymno 28310 29431 Sun–Thu 10am–3am, Fri–Sat 10am–4am

THE HAPPY WALKER

www.happywalker.com
The Happy Walker is a long established business that has an office in Rethymno. They specialize in hiking on Crete and organize different outings each day of the week.
G3 56 Tombazi, Rethymno 28310 52920

CULTURED CRETE

For a more restrained evening out, you'll find that Crete's main towns have some excellent modern art museums and galleries that are open quite late into the evening and that often exhibit the work of local artists and national figures. Some of the work can be hit and miss, but it's always entertaining. Music lovers should check for summer festivals and for outdoor classical music performances that can have a particular magic under the stars.

LIMNOUPOLIS WATER PARK

www.limnoupolis.gr
This big waterpark will keep the family happy with its waterslides, river rides, pools and other fun spots.
D3 Varipetro, 6.5km (4 miles) southwest of Chania 28210 33246 May–Oct daily 10–6 Six a day from Chania Expensive

NERATZIES MOSQUE CONCERTS

The splendid Neratzies Mosque is now a music school where public summer concerts are staged.
G3 Vernardou 1, Rethymno 28310 22724 Moderate

NOSTRALE

A café–bar on the old harbour waterfront, with a spacious interior and smart waterside terrace across the road. Runs with a mix of easy listening sounds and Greek rock.
G3 Plastira 7, Rethymno 28310 57858 Daily until late

THOLOS

Opened in 2010, Tholos is a terrific addition to Rethymno's music bar society. Great talk and good music, from jazz and blues to rock and reggae. Housed in an old Ottoman–Venetian building with much exposed stone and the domed *hammam* as a feature.
G3 N Foka 86, Rethymno 28310 50378

Restaurants

PRICES

Prices are approximate, based on a 3-course meal for one person.
€€€ over €25
€€ €15–€25
€ under €15

ALANA (€€€)
A leafy courtyard venue in Rethymno's old quarter, adds style to a fine menu of hot and cold starters, inventive salads and tasty mains such as pork with plums and pistachio nuts or fresh bream in lemon and olive oil dressing. The wine list is an excellent range of Cretan and Greek vintages.
G3 Salaminos 15, Rethymno 28310 27737
Daily dinner

AVLI (€€€)
It's worth splashing out for a meal at this elegant restaurant located within an old Venetian manor house. There's a delightful courtyard for outdoor dining. Signature dishes include grilled octopus and *fava* with caramelized beetroot.
G3 Odos Xanthoudidou 22, Rethymno
28310 26213
Daily dinner

THE BLUE HOUSE (€)
This south coast institution has views over Loutro's harbour and offers the best of fish dishes and Cretan cuisine in general. This is all enhanced by a friendly ambience and without the pointless veneer of many urban eateries. It also has good rooms available to rent.
E4 Loutro 28250 91127 Daily lunch and dinner

CAFÉ NUVEL (€)
A top location at the edge of Rethymno's old Venetian harbour makes this stylish café–bar a popular venue. Just right for treating yourself by day to low-fat baguettes, fresh crisp salads, mixed cold plates, or waffles and ice cream.
G3 Venetiko Limani, Rethymno 28310 52478
Daily until late

CASTELLO (€€)
At the heart of the old town of Rethymno, Castello offers Cretan and mainland Greek specialities with imaginative touches, such as shrimp with aniseed and veal with bacon, while sauces are delicious.
G3 Arabatzoglou 27, Rethymno 28310 50567
Daily dinner

SAY CHEESE

No one can visit Crete without sampling *myzithropitaki*, the delicious sweet cheese pies of the island. These little pastry envelopes are crammed with *myzithra* cheese, which is made from sheep or goat's milk. A higher proportion of whey to milk gives the cheese its softness, absence of salt gives it sweetness. As the cheese ages it dries and becomes harder and crumbly and is known as *anthotyros*. A sour version of this famous cheese is called *xynomizithra*.

COSMOS (€€€)
An award-winning restaurant with a balcony overlooking Platanias. For starters try the pies stuffed with cheese and spinach, or the Cretan sausages followed by fresh sea bass or *kokkinisto*, goat marinated in wine with a tomato-based sauce. There's a fine selection of Cretan and mainland wines to go with it all, and nostalgic piano playing can be heard on occasions.
D2 Platanias, Chania
69565 65813
Daily dinner

DIONYSOS (€€)
A popular and long-established taverna in this pleasant resort, Dionysos is noted for its good Cretan cooking. Browse the kitchen display for traditional dishes. Vegetarians can make good choices too.
C4 Venizelos, Palaiochora 28230 41243
Daily lunch and dinner

FAKA (€–€€)
Next to the old Venetian arsenals set back from

Chania's inner harbour, this solidly Cretan restaurant has a good selection of salads, starters and main dishes. The fish soup is very satisfying. In summer there's live Greek music most nights.
✚ D2 ✉ Old Arsenal, Chania ☎ 28210 42341 ⌚ Dinner daily

GEFIRA (€)
Just south of the river in Vryses, this café–bar has a big riverside terrace. It offers all types of drinks as well as sandwiches and snacks.
✚ E3 ✉ Vryses ☎ 28250 51556 ⌚ Daily 9am until early hours

KARIATIS (€€€)
Cretan-Italian cuisine is the style at this plush restaurant at the heart of Chania. Choose from a swathe of fine dishes such as salmon and avocado, fillet of beef with porcini mushrooms or chicken mozzarella, accompanied by a fine selection of Greek and world wines.
✚ D2 ✉ Platia Katehaki 12, Chania ☎ 28210 55600 ⌚ Daily dinner

KARNAGIO (€€)
This popular eatery, near Chania's Venetian arsenals, offers sturdy Cretan standards with added flair such as grilled small fish with the extra subtleties of Cretan soft cheese and honey.
✚ D2 ✉ Platia Katehaki 8, Chania ☎ 28210 53366 ⌚ Daily lunch and dinner Apr–Oct

KYRIA MARIA (€–€€)
This reliable, good-value favourite, close to the Rimondi Fountain, serves excellent Cretan grills and casseroles, plus good vegetarian choices, without any fuss but with a friendly attitude. The house wine provides the ideal accompaniment.
✚ G3 ✉ Moshovitou 20, Rethymno ☎ 28310 29078 ⌚ Daily dinner

METHEXIS (€–€€)
A big, friendly taverna in a good spot on Palaiochora's east side waterfront. The Cretan specialities range from delicious soups to fish dishes, including squid in ink sauce, as well as meat dishes and tasty standards such as *dolmadhes*. The house wine is very persuasive.
✚ C4 ✉ Palaiochora ☎ 28230 41431 ⌚ Daily lunch and dinner

EAT CRETE

Crete has numerous dishes, which although essentially Greek in substance are Cretan in style. Enhance your Greek salad experience with Cretan *dakos*, a hard rusk softened by tomatoes, feta and olive oil. *Kakavia* is a typically Cretan fish soup, though it's more of a thick stew flavoured with lemon and herbs. Vegetarians can delight in *ladera*, baked or stewed vegetables with rice.

MILIA (€€)
Whether staying at Milia (▷ 110) or not, a visit to the restaurant is worthwhile, especially for the home-grown and organic food prepared in wood-burning ovens. Favourites are potato, chestnut and onion stew, and rabbit in *mizithra* cheese.
✚ B3 ✉ Vlatos, Kissamos ☎ 28220 51569 ⌚ Daily lunch and dinner

MYLOS TOU KERATA (€–€€)
This popular taverna is in a one-time inn where a watermill once operated. A speciality is *boureki* (potatoes, courgettes and cheese in filo pastry) and there's a great range of charcoal grilled meats.
✚ D2 ✉ Platanias, 12km (7 miles) west of Chania ☎ 28210 68578 ⌚ All Day

NIKTERIDA (€€€)
The actor Anthony Quinn is said to have been taught the *syrtaki* (Zorba's dance) at this long-established restaurant located on the neck of the Akrotiri Peninsula. There are superb views across Souda Bay from the garden. Traditional starters, grilled meats and pasta feature strongly.
✚ D2 ✉ Korakies, Chania ☎ 28210 64215 ⌚ Daily lunch and dinner

PALAIOS MILOS (VIEUX MOULIN) (€€)
The 'Old Mill' is down among the fabulous waterland of Argiroupoli; among the plane and chestnut trees where the muted roar of falling water is music enough to accompany excellent grilled meat and local trout dishes.
F4 Argiroupoli 28310 81209 Daily lunch and dinner

SAFRAN (€€)
An old Venetian building contains a modern interior at this fine restaurant on Chania's inner harbour. A variety of salads are good openers for tasty pastas and risotto, with seafood ingredients to the fore.
D2 Akti Tombazi 30, Chania 28210 56333 Daily lunch and dinner

TAMAM (€€)
The very popular Tamam is located in part of Chania's old Turkish *hammam*, the baths, and fittingly offers a range of great Greek, Cretan, Turkish and Arabic specialities all cooked with subtlety.
D2 Odos Zambeliou 49, Chania 28210 96080 Daily lunch and dinner

THALASSOGRAFIA (€€€)
Location cannot be bettered at this popular place on a series of terraces above the sea road and beneath the walls of the Fortezza. Traditional Cretan and modern Mediterranean cuisine.
G3 Kefalogiannidon 33, Rethymno 28310 52569 All day

TO PIGADI (€€)
Translating as 'The Well', this little restaurant has good Cretan cuisine with a wider Mediterranean flair. Try mussels *saganaki* with hot peppers and pasta, chicken fillet in a sauce of Cretan sheep's cheese on a bed of pasta, or a seafood spread of squid, octopus, cuttlefish and small fish with barley pasta.
G3 Xanthoudidou 31, Rethymno 28310 27522 Apr–Oct daily 1pm–midnight; Nov–Mar Tue–Sat 6pm–midnight, Sun 1pm–midnight

JUST DESSERTS

The concept of 'dessert' is not traditional in Greece, where *mezédhes*, vegetables and staples of meat and fish are the welcome mainstay in villages and where specialist cake shops cater separately for the Greek sweet tooth. Many top-end restaurants now offer deliciously creative desserts, however, and the more traditional delights such as *giaourti kai meli* (yoghurt with honey) make for a tasty end to any meal.

VENETO (€€€)
Located in what was once part of a monastery, the Veneto is Rethymno dining at its finest; Cretan cuisine with added international flair. Start with oven-baked Sfakian meat and cheese cake followed by young goat with *stamnagathi*, a type of chicory, or fresh fish of the day. The wine list is outstanding, easily one of the best in Crete, if not beyond.
G3 Epimenidou 4, Rethymno 28310 56634 May–Oct daily dinner

WELL OF THE TURK (€€–€€€)
Subtle fusion of North African and Mediterranean cuisine has made this long-established eatery a firm favourite. The historic surroundings, including the eponymous well, match the style
D2 K Sarpaki 1–3, Chania 28210 54547 Wed–Mon dinner

XANI (€€)
Opposite the picturesque Jewish Synagogue, is this classic Cretan restaurant conjuring such great dishes as *marathopita*, fennel pie, chicken and prunes, or fresh fish. Live music is likely to fire up at any time.
D2 Parados Kondalaki, Chania 28210 75795 Daily 11–midnight

Central Crete is where the ancient world really takes hold of your soul. It's where the most dramatic archaeological sites lie, and where the island's mountains soar to their highest point at the mighty peak of Psiloritis.

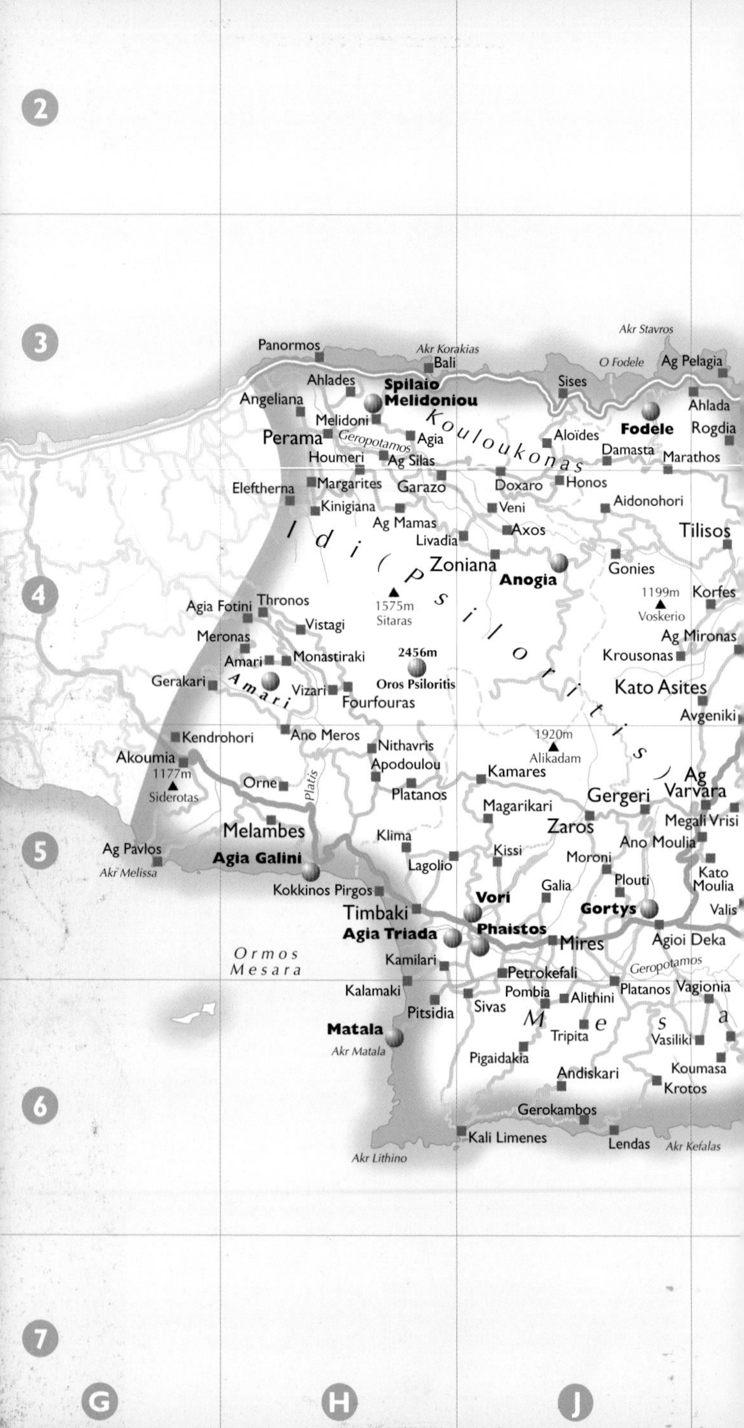

2
3
4
5
6
7
G
H
J
Panormos
Akr Korakias
Bali
Akr Stavros
O Fodele
Ag Pelagia
Ahlades
Spilaio Melidoniou
Sises
Angeliana
Ahlada
Melidoni
Kouloukonas
Fodele
Rogdia
Perama
Geropotamos
Agia
Aloïdes
Damasta
Marathos
Houmeri
Ag Silas
Eleftherna
Margarites
Garazo
Doxaro
Honos
Kinigiana
Veni
Aidonohori
Ag Mamas
Axos
Tilisos
Livadia
Idi (Psiloritis)
Zoniana
Gonies
Anogia
1575m
Sitaras
1199m
Voskerio
Korfes
Agia Fotini
Thronos
Vistagi
Ag Mironas
Meronas
2456m
Oros Psiloritis
Krousonas
Amari
Monastiraki
Gerakari
Amari
Vizari
Fourfouras
Kato Asites
Avgeniki
Kendrohori
Ano Meros
1920m
Alikadam
Akoumia
1177m
Siderotas
Nithavris
Apodoulou
Kamares
Orne
Platis
Platanos
Ag Varvara
Gergeri
Magarikari
Megali Vrisi
Melambes
Zaros
Klima
Ano Moulia
Ag Pavlos
Akr Melissa
Agia Galini
Kissi
Moroni
Lagolio
Kato Moulia
Kokkinos Pirgos
Galia
Plouti
Vori
Gortys
Valis
Timbaki
Phaistos
Agia Triada
Mires
Agioi Deka
Ormos Mesara
Kamilari
Geropotamos
Petrokefali
Kalamaki
Pombia
Alithini
Platanos
Vagionia
Pitsidia
Sivas
Mesara
Tripita
Vasiliki
Matala
Akr Matala
Pigaidakia
Andiskari
Koumasa
Krotos
Gerokambos
Kali Limenes
Lendas
Akr Kefalas
Akr Lithino

0
20 km
0
10 miles
Kolpos
Irakliou
Akr Panagia
Ammoudara
Gazi
Arolithos
Kavrohori
Knossos
Kato Kalesia
Silamos
Voutes
Stavrakia
Ag Sillas
Dafnes
Giorifos
Pano
Arhanes
Venerato
Prof Ilias
Kiparissos
Karkadiotissa
Ag Thomas
Genna
Larani
Metaxohori
Melidohori
Tefeli
Inia
Ligortinos
Faragiana
Loures
Asimi
Protoria
Sternes
Harakas
Pirgos
Loukia
Kofina
Platanias
Paranimfi
Kapetaniana
Tris Ekklisies
Akr Martelos
Gournes
Cretaquarium
Akr Hersonisos
Limenas Chersonisou
Hersonisos
Lychnostatis
Elea
Anopoli
Skalani
Ag Ioannis
Aïtania
Galipe
Haraso
Kalo Horio
Episkopi
Potamies
Kounavi
Myrtia
Apostoli
Ag Paraskies
Kastelli
Houdetsi
Voni
Zofori
Kastamonitsa
Thrapsano
Alagnio
Roussohoria
Patsideros
Geraki
Panorama
Arkalohori
Nipiditos
Partira
Kato Poulies
Panagia
Badias
Ini
Afrati
Thomadiano
Karavados
Garipa
Martha
Kalivia
Skinias
Kefalados
Anapodiaris
Hondros
Kato Kastelliana
Demati
Mesohorio
Keratokambos
Tsoutsouros
Ethia
O Keratokambou
K
L
M

Agia Triada

The Psiloritis range are a perfect backdrop (left); detail of a sarcophagus (right)

THE BASICS

H5
3km (2 miles) west of Phaistos
28920 91360
Jul–Oct daily 8–7.30; Nov–Jun Tue–Sun 8.30–3
Café at Phaistos (€)
Only as far as Phaistos (3km/2miles)
Moderate

HIGHLIGHTS

- Tranquil location
- A cohesive impression of a Minoan settlement
- Less crowded

TIP

- Whether before or after a visit to Agia Triada, be sure to visit Iraklio's Archaeological Museum to check out frescoes and artefacts from the site.

This Minoan summer palace is where the idyllic lifestyle of a Greek Golden Age reached its apogee, and where top Minoans are said to have debunked for the summer months.

Summer retreat Agia Triada (named after the Holy Trinity, a much later Byzantine chapel overlooking the site) lies a dry and dusty 3km (2 miles) west of the major Minoan site of Phaistos (▷ 78) along a narrow surfaced road. The site was certainly viable in terms of location and commerce. It lies on the slope of an idyllic hill that is dense with greenery. During the Minoan period the sea reached the base of the hill, and a cobbled harbour road can be seen today descending from the palace to the overgrown shoreline. The complex includes the remains of a row of what were probably shops and storerooms and a small village.

Distinctive artwork What Agia Triada lacks in size compared with other major Minoan sites, it makes up for in the richness of the artefacts found here. The Minoans developed a sophisticated style of painting frescoes, and Agia Triada has yielded some of the finest examples of the period, although much reconstruction was required. The animals and people featured in the frescoes are entirely natural and unwarlike, suggesting a true Golden Age of peace and plenty. Outstanding objects found here include the Harvester Vase and Boxer Vase (held at Iraklio's Archaeological Museum (▷ 24–25).

The thrilling shark tank (left); a colourful, mysterous sea anemone (right)

Cretaquarium

You've swum in Crete's warm, azure waters, now take a peep into the marine wonderland of the Mediterranean at the fascinating Cretaquarium—without even getting your feet wet.

Thrilling experience The Cretaquarium is one of the largest aquariums in Europe. Part of the Hellenic Centre for Marine Research, in its collection of sixty tanks the fascinating and diverse seascape of the Mediterranean is brought to life. The tanks range in size from huge installations in which sharks and other large species cruise happily together, to small tanks containing exquisite seahorses and brilliant sea anemones. Spiny lobsters, conger eels and Moray eels, groupers and scorpion fish are only a few of the hundreds of Mediterranean and tropical species on display in this magical marine environment.

Information points Information is well organized throughout the galleries, and there are touchscreen points in various languages to help you interpret the aspects of marine ecosystems. Video projectors and other state-of-the-art devices enhance the experience and an easy-to-use audio guide, with a choice of nine languages, gives in-depth details on how the marine world functions. Pools enable you to handle certain species without damaging them. There is a gift shop with souvenirs and fine jewellery, but also books and artefacts of educational value. A stone's throw from the aquarium is the Aegean, uncurling onto sandy beaches.

THE BASICS

www.cretaquarium.gr
L4
Former American base at Gournes, 14km (9 miles) east of Iraklio
28103 37788
Jun–Sep daily 9–9; Oct–May 9–7
Café–restaurant (€–€€)
Regular service daily from Iraklio and Malia
Excellent
Expensive

HIGHLIGHTS

- The tank of jellyfish
- The Big Boys' tank (sharks)
- Hands-on pools
- Seaside location

TIP

- Call in at the International Exhibition Centre of Crete, on the approach to the Cretaquarium. This is another fine modern building that stages major cultural exhibitions.

Gortys

TOP 25

HIGHLIGHTS

- The engraved stones of the Law Codes
- Roman remains
- Basilica of St. Titus

TIP

- To reach the Roman ruins, walk for 200m (218 yards) beside an extremely busy road. Cross, with great care, and follow a cobbled path to reach the fenced ruins of a substantial Roman pantheon, with other scattered remains beyond.

The high point of the scattered ancient site of Gortys is a law code that will make your toes curl with its Draconian rules that favour the rich and high born. It's written in stone, literally.

A long history The kingdom of Gortys was formerly the capital of a post-Minoan Crete, which extended its influence throughout the Aegean and into North Africa. The ancient site lies scattered over a wide area. A Minoan-era settlement existed here and later flourished under the Dorians, the successors to the Mycenaeans. Gortys had ousted Phaistos (▷ 78) from its ascendancy by the third century BC and the city reached its apogee as the capital of Crete after the Roman invasion of 67BC. During AD824, the Muslim invaders

Clockwise from far top left: The Law Codes of Gortys engraved on rock in the Odeon; the apse of the basilica of St. Titus; Gortys' semi-circular Roman Odeon

from Southern Spain destroyed Gortys and the site was never recolonized.

Monumental building First is the important apse of the sixth-century Basilica of St. Titus, who is said to have brought Christianity to the island and was martyred here for his pains. Near by is the semicircular Roman Odeon. Behind the Odeon, now protected by a brick arcade, is Gortys' greatest treasure, huge stone blocks engraved with the famous Law Code of Gortys of 480–460BC, the first known code of law in Europe. Written in archaic Dorian dialect, the lines follow the mind-boggling, ancient form with lines written from right to left on one line, then from left to right on the next. The code deals with hierarchical civil issues such as divorce, adultery, inheritance and property rights.

THE BASICS

J5

Agia Deka 46km (28 miles) south of Iraklio

28920 31144

Apr–Oct daily 8–7; Nov–Mar 8–3

Café–bar (€)

Regular service daily from Iraklio

Few

Moderate; free on Sun in winter (access is free to the Roman ruins in olive groves on the south side of the main road)

Knossos

TOP 25

HIGHLIGHTS

- Frescoes
- Throne Room
- Queen's Suite
- Piano Nobile
- Bull Relief

TIP

- If you can bat away the often persistent guides, head straight for the large open area of the Central Court from where information panels give a reasonable indication of the best way round the site.

Knossos is a remarkable fusion of awesome archaeology and showmanship with just a whiff of theme-park history. It is an irresistible experience all the same, a dramatic insight into how the other half lived in a true Golden Age.

Major sight Knossos attracts huge crowds of visitors including cruise-ship groups and organized parties, all of which can make a visit something of a gruelling experience. Yet, Knossos imparts a powerful impression of Minoan civilization in its finest hour. It was here that the Minoans are said to have established their largest 'palace' community in all of Crete. It is also where the enigma of the Minoans began to be resolved in 1894 by the enthusiastic British archaeologist Arthur Evans. Excavations,

There are many remarkable frescoes and murals decorating the walls throughout the ruins at Knossos, some of which have been restored to their original colours

which began in 1900, revealed 13,000sq m (139,930sq ft) of significant buildings surrounded by a town that supported around 12,000 inhabitants.

Legendary king Evans made several sweeping assumptions about Knossos, not least the conviction that the labyrinthine layout and the sacred symbols on walls and pillars suggested that here was the palace of the legendary King Minos and the lair of the mythological Minotaur. From these heady assumptions, Evans gave the name Minoan to the fabulous culture he uncovered. The complex is not huge, but every individual feature, including the reconstructed Throne Room, Piano Nobile, Royal Apartments, the Prince—or Princess—of the Lilies fresco and the Bull Relief are fascinating.

THE BASICS

K4

5km (3 miles) south of Iraklio

28102 31940

Apr–Sep daily 8–7.30; Oct–Mar 8.30–3

Café-restaurant (€€)

No. 2 from Iraklio's Bus Station A every 30 mins

Good (as far as the main court)

Expensive; combined ticket available with Iraklio's Archaiologiko Mouseio (▷ 24–25)

Phaistos

TOP 25

HIGHLIGHTS

- Great location
- Glorious views
- The Grand Staircase
- Royal apartments

TIP

- The famous Phaistos Disc, now in Iraklio's Archaeological Museum (▷ 24), was a major discovery. Small, round and made of clay, the disc is inscribed with spiralling pictographs that defy translation.

The Minoan palace and city of Phaistos was said to have been ruled by King Minos' brother Rhadamanthys—who must have had a very good eye for rooms with a view.

Major settlement Phaistos was probably as important as Knossos although it developed later than Evans' iconic find. An original palace was destroyed in 1700BC and was replaced by a second palace, which was destroyed in turn in 1450BC when most Minoan settlements seem to have been destroyed by fire. Excavations were carried out here by the Italian Federico Halbherr close to the time Arthur Evans was working at Knossos. Halbherr's approach was far more rigorous, however, and he has left us a site, which, although lacking the reconstructions

Clockwise from far left: Rows of seats in the ancient theatre, with the Grand Staircase beyond; glorious views from Phaistos over olive groves to Mount Psiloritis; the Grand Staircase; store rooms (magazine) for the giant pithoi (storage jars); giant pithoi uncovered at Phaistos

and cohesion of Knossos, is somehow more persuasive and satisfying.

Steps and stones Steps lead down to the right of the entrance into the West Court and theatrical area, via an upper court. Stone pits to the south of the West Court were probably used for storing grain. From the West Court a major feature, the Grand Staircase, leads up to the Central Court at the heart of the complex. To the north of the Central Court are the Royal Apartments, which have protective roofing sheets and are fenced off to prevent erosion. You can still view their cool, shadowy interiors and let your imagination roam. The stonework at Phaistos has a rich patina and has not been disturbed by too much reconstruction. Above all, the open, airy location helps ease the pressure of the crowds.

THE BASICS

J5

Phaistos (66km/40 miles southwest of Iraklio)

28920 42315

Jun–Oct daily 8–7.30; Nov–May 8–5.30

Café (€)

Regular service from Iraklio Bus Station B

None (numerous steps)

Expensive

Oros Psiloritis

Visitors look down into the Ideon Cave (left); the road leading to the cave (right)

THE BASICS

H4
17km (11 miles) south of Anogia to base of mountain
None; take food and plenty of water
None

HIGHLIGHTS

- The Ideon Cave
- Rugged countryside
- Clear mountain air
- Great mountain walks

TIP

- The hike to the summit of Psiloritis is fairly straightforward but should not be tackled without sturdy boots and weatherproof clothing, plenty of food and water and good experience of route finding.

You can hardly miss Crete's highest mountain. The mighty Psiloritis dominates almost every twist and turn of the roads, and in winter and spring its snowcapped summit glistens in the sun.

Dramatic Crete's highest mountain can be approached on its northern side by a wide surfaced road that snakes through a dramatic rock-studded wilderness for 21km (13 miles) beyond Anogia (▷ 81). The road ends on the Nida Plain, 1,000m (328ft) or so below the summit of Psiloritis at a rather run down and largely unused visitor centre and a more cheerful summer café–taverna. At 2,456m (8,055ft), Mount Psiloritis, or Mount Ida, is the highest point on Crete. Its northern side is a barren and stony wilderness with few green areas other than the rather washed out Nida Plain.

Hard hike It's a gruelling 7–8 hour return hike from the road end to the summit of Psiloritis. For the less able a short uphill trudge from the road end takes you to the Ideon Andron (Ideon Cave, also known to as the Ida Cave), a claimant along with the Dikteon Cave (▷ 98) for the title of birthplace of Zeus. Excavations in the 1880s yielded bronze shields from the ninth and eighth centuries BC, suggesting that the cave was a post-Minoan cult centre. You can walk down into the interior of the cave, but it is fairly shallow with no dramatic natural rock formations. The rusty tramlines and wooden timbering are remnants of archaeological work.

More to See

AGIA GALINI

The friendly resort of Agia Galini rambles down a broad fold in the hills of Crete's central south coast, twisting and turning happily until opening onto a busy little harbour. It can get crowded in summer and only has a small local beach. There are plenty of good tavernas, restaurants, cafés and bars, however, and all modern services.

H5 54km (33 miles) southeast of Rethymno Cafés, bars and tavernas in the village Regular service daily from Iraklio Bus Station B and from Rethymno Few

AMARI VALLEY

The Amari Valley lies on the west side of Mount Psiloritis and is very broad, green and fertile. Olives, cherries, pears and figs are grown here. Amari was famed as a centre of fierce resistance to German occupation in the 1940s and many of its villages, including Gerakari, Meronas and Ano Meros, were burned and then razed by the Germans as reprisal for resistance. Today, the serenity of Amari is memorial enough to that brave resistance.

H4 Amari Valley Village *kafenion* and tavernas Three Mon, Wed and Fri, two Sat, one Sun, from Rethymno Few

ANOGIA

The name of Crete's highest village translates fittingly as the 'Upper Earth', a romantic evocation that does not match Anogia's harsh past. Ever resilient against invaders, the village suffered vicious reprisals, because of resistance to German occupation. Every able-bodied male that could be rounded up was executed and all buildings were flattened. The rebuilt village has thus lost much of its traditional architectural character, but today it throbs with all the cheerful bustle of everyday rural life. Anogia is noted for weaving and embroidery.

J4 Anogia Many cafés and tavernas Four Mon–Sat, two Sun, from Iraklio Bus Station B; two Mon–Fri from Rethymno Few

Agia Galini harbour

Gerakari's village church engulfed by cherry blossom, in the Amari Valley

FODELE

Fodele claims to be the birthplace of the painter Domenico Theotokopoulos, immortalized by his Spanish name of El Greco, in spite of academic arguments that Crete's famous painter was born in Iraklio. Fodele is a pretty place and linen, lace and embroidery, as well as local oranges and lemons, are for sale in shops and on stalls. The El Greco House (Spiti El Greco; tel 2810 521500; May–Oct Tue–Sun 9–5) is opposite the Byzantine Church of the Panagia.

J3 · 19km (12 miles) northwest of Iraklio · Taverna El Greco (€) · Two a day from Iraklio Bus Station B · None

LYCHNOSTATIS OPEN AIR MUSEUM

This informative and entertaining folk museum is located about 20km (12 miles) east of Iraklio. There are convincing recreations of traditional Cretan buildings, including a farmhouse, olive press, windmill and shepherd's shelter. Displays include farming implements, village crafts, orchards and herb plots. There is also a varied programme of traditional music and dance events. Check for guided tours in various languages.

M4 · Limenas Chersonisou · 28970 23660 · Sun–Fri 9–2 · Café (€) · Good · Moderate

MATALA

Celebrity footprints leave deep marks in the sands of Matala, where 1960s hippies dropped out to live the laid-back life in the resort's cliff caves above golden sands. Musicians Bob Dylan and Joni Mitchell are said to have dropped in and out; the latter even featured Matala in song. The caves are now fenced off and designated as archaeological sites, because of their possible history as Roman and early Christian tombs.

H6 · 70km (43 miles) southwest of Iraklio · Caves daily 11.30–7 · Cafés and tavernas on the beach · Three a day Mon–Fri, five Sat, two Sun,

Statue of El Greco beside the museum in Fodele

A traditional Cretan church, Lychnostatis Open Air Museum

from Iraklio Bus Station B and from Mires
Caves moderate

MYRTIA

While Fodele (▷ 82) claims El Greco, the flower-filled Myrtia claims the great writer Nikos Kazantzakis (1883–1957) whose parents lived in a large house in the village's central *platia*, although Kazantzakis was born in Iraklio. The house is now a museum (tel 02810 742451; Mar–Oct daily 9–7; Nov–Feb Sun 10–3) dedicated to the writer.

L4 16km (10 miles) southeast of Iraklio Cafés and tavernas on the *platia* Five a day Mon–Fri from Iraklio Bus Station B (Agia Galini bus)

SPILAIO MELIDONIOU

Spilaio Melidoniou (Melidoni Cave) is on a hillside high above the agricultural town of Perama and has exhilarating views of Mount Psiloritis. The cave has some splendid thickets of stalactites and stalagmites and other lavish formations, but is haunted by the memory of an atrocity that took place in 1824 when about 370 local people, mostly women, children and the elderly, hid in the cave from Ottoman troops, who then lit fires and asphyxiated everyone inside.

H3 4km (2.5 miles) northeast of Perama, a short drive from the village of Melidoni 28340 22046 Apr–Nov daily 9–7 Café–bar by the cave entrance (€) Several daily from Rethymno, then a half-hour walk Few Moderate

VORI

Vori is home to the Ethnologiko Mouseio Kritis (Museum of Cretan Ethnology; tel 28929 91110; Apr–Oct daily 10–6). In a modest building near the church, it covers all aspects of rural life in Crete, with sections on food, agriculture, weaving, pottery, metalwork, transportation and religion. There is an evocative section on the Cretan Resistance during World War II.

J5 4km (2.5 miles) north of Phaistos Tavernas Several daily from Iraklio Bus Station B

Buried in the hillside, the entrance to the Melidoni Cave

Basket display in the Museum of Cretan Ethnology, Vori

Shopping

ARCHAEOLOGICAL REPLICAS
At the major Minoan sites such as Knossos and Phaistos, the official site shops dispense a range of items including replica artefacts. These can be seriously expensive, especially so at Knossos, although prices for small items can be affordable.

AROLITHOS CRAFT VILLAGE
www.arolithosvillage.gr
Craftwork shops are part of this traditional Cretan village in the hills near Tilisos. Skilled people create pottery, wooden furniture, woven goods and silverware, all of which can be purchased.
K4 8km (5 miles) west of Iraklio on the Old National Road 28108 21050

BOTANO
Organic products are available at this outlet in the main square. They include Cretan *dakos*, (the Greek bruschetta), herbs from the Cretan mountains and from world sources, varieties of tea, health and beauty products, and frankincense from the monastic enclave of Mount Athos in Northern Greece
H6 Matala
28920 42295

DOMAIN ZACHARIOUDAKIS
Excellent wines are produced at this gravity-fed winery in the south of Central Crete. They include reds from Syrah and Merlot grapes, and whites from Vidiano and Sauvignon Blanc.
J5 Plouti, 1km (0.5 miles) north of Gortys
28920 24660 Tue–Sun 10–6

MARKETS AND MORE
On Saturday mornings there is an entertaining street market in the busy agricultural town of Mires, about 18km (11 miles) west of Agia Galini. On Thursday mornings there is a smaller market at Timbaki, 8km (5 miles) west of Agia Galini. You will find a range of fascinating domestic goods among the food stalls.

THE BIG BOYS

Scattered around many Minoan sites are the giant clay jars used by the Minoans and their successors for storing olive oil and wine. These are known as *pithoi*. The village of Thrapsano, southeast of Iraklio, has a long tradition of pottery making and is said to have supplied Minoan Knossos with its storage jars. Today *pithoi* and smaller pots are still made at Thrapsano, but for decorative use. If you fancy a mightily visible memory of Crete in your garden you can have one of these giant vessels shipped from Crete.

MINOS
The Minos winery is at the centre of Cretan vine growing, offering a range of products including wine, olive oil, olive soap, honey, herbs and spices.
L4 Peza, 17km (10 miles) south of Iraklio
28107 41213 Mon–Fri 9–4, Sat 11–4

TARRAH GLASS
This glass-making workshop and gallery, run by a talented husband- and wife-team of glassmakers, makes a delightful balance to Anogia's well-known woven goods and embroidery trade.
J4 Anogia (on the road to Iraklio) 28340 31357

VOLYRAKIS POTTERY
The village of Thrapsano (▷ panel) is where you can order yourself a giant clay pot, a modern equivalent of the Minoan *pithoi*, the giant clay containers used in ancient times for storing olive oil and wine.
L4 Thrapsano, 28km (17 miles) southeast of Iraklio
28910 41699

WEAVING AND EMBROIDERY
The villages of Anogia (▷ 81) and Fodele (▷ 82) are noted for fine embroidery and woven goods. There are workshops in Anogia, and in both villages street stalls display the wares during summer.

Entertainment and Activities

AKOUNA MATATA

On the southern side of Matala's beach is this popular bar devoted to rock and reggae and to good times generally. It also serves up good fish and meat dishes from the grill.

H6 Matala 69473 43688 All day until late

AROLITHOS

www.arolithosvillage.gr

Cretan evenings with live music and dancing in full traditional costume take place in this cleverly constructed authentic Cretan village in the hills near Tilisos. You can watch the local artisans at work in their workshops and buy the handmade goods that take your eye.

K4 8km (5 miles) west of Iraklio on the Old National Road 28108 21050

BRAVO PARK WATER AND PLAY PARK

www.bravopark.gr

Pools, waterslides, play areas and much more keep the youngsters happy at this fun place west of Iraklio, while parents relax poolside.

K4 Ammoudara 28310 19334 Apr–Oct

CAMELOT

Eat your heart out young Lancelot, this faux-castle club has long drawn lively clubbers, mainly visitors, with its full on sounds.

M4 Odos Minoos 9, Limenas Chersonisou 28970 22734

KAROUZANOS EVENING

www.karouzanos.gr

Live the traditional Cretan life for an evening at the mountain village of Karouzanos. Evenings kick off with a glass of raki, followed by a stroll round the village and then dinner in a local taverna, to the accompaniment of traditional music and dance.

L4 Kato Karouzana, 10km (6 miles) south of Limenas Chersonisou 28910 28413

MILESTONE BLUES & JAZZ BAR

Relax with drinks and good conversation at this summertime venue, with its background of great music from a large and eclectic collection of CDs.

H5 Agia Galini

LOVELY *LYRA*

There is no finer sound in Crete than the exhilarating notes of a *lyra*, the traditional stringed instrument of the island. The *lyra* is a small three-stringed fiddle with a pear-shaped body, played with a bow. It is either rested on the knee or simply held against the chest, and the notes are created by the player pressing the backs of the nails against the strings. Impromptu sessions often held in village *kafenions* or tavernas are truly unforgettable experiences.

28230 91519 Summer 5pm–early hours

ODYSSEIA STABLES

www.horseriding.gr

In the foothills of the Dikti Mountains, these riding stables organize a series of tailored rides for beginners to experienced riders, and include a six-day trek across the mountains and the Lasithiou Plateau.

M4 Avdou 28970 51080

WATER CITY

www.watercity.gr

Billed as Crete's biggest water park, this sprawling complex boasts huge waterslides and covered chutes, numerous pools for all tastes and abilities, including a wave pool, and plenty of water-based games and activities for all. There are bars, restaurants, shops and a range of other services.

L4 Anapoli, 14km (9 miles) east of Iraklio 28107 81316-7 Apr–Sep daily 10–7 Regular service from Iraklio and Malia Good

ZERVAS WATERSPORTS

For all kinds of beach fun and sports at the resort of Stalida, just west of Malia, the Zervas Beach hotel has a beach station offering everything from pedaloes to waterskiing and parasailing.

M4 Stalida, 28km (17 miles) east of Iraklio 28970 32993

Restaurants

PRICES

Prices are approximate, based on a 3-course meal for one person.

€€€	over €25
€€	€15–€25
€	under €15

ARAVANES TAVERNA (€€)

At the heart of the Amari Valley (▷ 81) in a tiny village, this classic taverna serves Cretan food at its best, with meat and fresh vegetables to the fore. Every now and then they have exuberant musical evenings.

H4 Thronos, Amari Valley 28330 22760 Daily lunch and dinner

O BELGOU (€)

Classic village food such as authentic *mezedhes* and other Cretan specialities are on offer at the heart of Vori.

J5 Vori 28920 91182 All day

CAFÉ PLATIA (€)

A very popular café-cum-bistro, this is the place for healthy eating breakfasts, snacks and salads. The ice cream is very welcome during the day and the cocktails at night.

H5 Harbourfront, Agia Galini 28320 91185 Daily 8–2, 6–late

CRETA (€–€€)

A longstanding favourite, this eatery does not disappoint with its traditional meat and fish dishes. You can either select from the kitchen trays or eat straight from the grill.

M4 Kaniadaki 4, Limenas Chersonisou 28790 24138 Daily lunch and dinner

O FAROS (€–€€)

As Cretan as you'll get, O Faros is a small taverna with no fancy terrace, apart from a couple of streetside tables. It's halfway up a narrow street just west of Agia Galini's main street. Kyria Maria is in the kitchen conjuring great fish treats, and is also happy to rustle up meat or spaghetti dishes and the usual *mezedhes*. If you're looking for something special like *astakos* (lobster) you'll need to order the day before. Also good Cretan wines such as Calliga or Athiri.

H5 Agia Galini 28320 91346 Daily lunch and dinner

RAKI

You may find yourself presented with a complimentary glass of the Cretan 'firewater', raki, or *tsikoudia* at the end of your meal, usually accompanied by a small cake or *glika tou koutaliou* (spoon sweet), the rinds of fruit such as oranges, lemons, whole cherries or grapes, and even rose petals, softened in a rich syrup. Raki is distilled from the skin and pips of grapes after wine extraction and is traditionally taken at one gulp. It has power–avoid, if driving.

GIALOS (€)

The long line of café–bars, with glassed terraces overlooking the water, along the west end of the Plakias seafront are much of a muchness. But Gialos, the last in line, overlooks the small harbour and has a good atmosphere to go with all types of drinks and snacks.

F4/5 Plakias 28320 32235 All day

KALESMA (€€)

You're never short of eating places in Malia, but for something better than the standard places try this *mezedopoulio* that specializes in plates of the Greek *mezedhes*.

M4 Omirou 8 (Malia old town) 28970 33125 Daily lunch and dinner

SCALA (€€)

Where Matala takes to the low cliff on the south side of the village, you'll find this resolutely local fish restaurant where they offer local caught species such as *bourbounia* (red mullet) and calamari. Enjoy the wine also, but perhaps carry a small torch for negotiating the mildly rough ground, on the way back to civilization in the dark

H6 Matala 28920 45489 Daily dinner

Go east for a less crowded Crete, to vibrant resort towns, dramatic mountains and compelling Minoan remains. Add to this some fine beaches, timeless villages, remote monasteries and friendly people.

2
3
4
5
6
7
M
N
P
Akr Drepani
Vlihadia
Akr Ag Ioannis
Paralia Milatou
Amigdalia
Anogia
Skinias
Vrouhas
Sisi
Milatos
Nofalias
Karidi
Plaka
Stalida
Malia
Spinalonga
Vrachasi
718m
Loutsi
Elounda
Mochos
Neapoli
Limnes
Akr Vagia
Avdou
Kera
Houmeriakos
Selena
Zenia
Pinakiano
Tzermiado
Nisi Psira
Tapes
Flamouriana
Agios Nikolaos
Mesa Lasithi
1663m
Lasithiou
Lato
Mohlos
Katharo Tsivi
Ammoudara
Plati
Psihro
Kolpos Mirambellou
Dikteon Andron
Agios Georgios
Panagia Kera
Platanos
Kaminaki
Lastros
Avdeliakos
1485m
Kroustas
Istro
Dikti
Platia Korifi
Pahia Ammos
Kavousi
Kalo Horio
Gournia
Katofigi
2141m
Selakano
Prina
Thriptis
Afendis Hristos
Kalamafka
Meseleri
Monastiraki
Orino
Ano Viannos
Metaxohori
Males
Makrilia
Stavros
Ag Ioannis
Amiras
Simi
Anatoli
Kato Horio
Mavros Kolimbos
Riza
Mournies
Kendri
Vaïnia
Ag Vasilios
Gra Ligia
Ferma
Ammoudares
Sikologos
Arvi
Tertsa
Mirtos
Nea Mirtos
Ierapetra
Akr Sidonia

0
20 km
0
10 miles
Akr Sideros
Akr Mavros
Nisi Elasa
Vai
O Grandes
Akr Faneromeni
Akr Vamvakia
Moni Toplou
Papadiokambos
O Sitias
Nisi Grandes
Sitia
Palekastro
Akr Plaka
Ag Fotia
Lidia
Angathias
Hamezi
Skopi
Piskokefalo
Mirsini
Exo Mouliana
Stavromenos
803m
Prinias
Mitato
Langada
O Karoumbes
Tourloti
Sfaka
Sfakia
Epano Episkopi
Katsidoni
Akr Avlaki
Orno
1238 m
Askordalia
Skordilo
Dafni
Nea Presos
Sitanos
Zakros
Zakros Palati
Sikea
F Nekron
Kato Zakros
Akr Zakros
Hrisopigi
Papagiannades
Vori
Handras
Lamnoni
Stavrohori
Lithines
Ziros
Ag Stefanos
Armeni
Hametoulo
Makrygialos
Perivolakia
Xerokambos
Analipsi
Kalo Horio
Koutsouras
Ag Triada
Nisi Kavalli
Goudouras
Atherinolakkos
Akr Goudoura
Q
R
S

Agios Nikolaos

HIGHLIGHTS

- Archaeological Museum
- Folk Museum
- People watching
- Strolling the waterfront

TIP

- Call in at Agios Nikolaos's modest Municipal Art Gallery on the second floor of a charming 19th-century mansion. Exhibitions often feature quite challenging works by contemporary Greek artists.
✉ Oktobriou 28 ☎ 28410 26899 ◷ Daily 11–2, 6–9

Once the port for the ancient Greek settlement of Lato (▷ 99), today Agios Nikolaos has more charm than most towns of its size. It's busy enough, but somehow manages to maintain a laid-back, soothing pace of life.

Beautiful view The Venetians built a fortress at Agios Nikolaos to command the Gulf of Mirabello 'the beautiful view'. Nothing remained of the fort after Ottoman destruction and an earthquake in 1995, and the modern town was later named after the nearby Byzantine church of Agios Nikolaos. Today Agios Nikolaos is the capital of Lasithiou Province, and although it has no major architectural features, its charm is inescapable. At its heart lies an intriguing central lagoon, Lake Voulismeni, a circular sea inlet that

Clockwise from left: Lake Voulismeni provides a stunning setting for Agios Nikolaos; displays inside the Archaeological Museum; Kitroplatia beach

is linked to the outer harbour by a short channel spanned by a bridge. The town's excellent Archaeological Museum includes the exquisite Goddess of Mirtos figurine-cum-vessel.

Perfect base The Folk Museum beside Lake Voulismeni is a delight; next door is the Tourist Information Office. Southeast of the harbour is the tiny beach of Kitroplatia, and a busy yacht marina with another beach beyond it. For a much better beach experience, head for the sandy strand at Almiros, 2km (1 mile) to the south. The town is the perfect base for exploring Eastern Crete. In the evening the centre becomes something of a fashion catwalk linking the stylish cafés, bars and restaurants that line the lagoon and harbourfront, and the friendly, relaxed ambience is welcoming to all.

THE BASICS

N4

Harbour cafés and tavernas

Regular service to Iraklio, Malia, Limin Hersonisos, Sitia and Ierapetra

Few

Akti I Koundourou 20; tel 28410 22357

Elounda and Spinalonga

Elounda harbour (left); silhouette of Spinalonga at dawn (right)

THE BASICS

N4/P4
7km (4 miles) north of Agios Nikolaos
Cafés and restaurants around the harbour
Regular service from Agios Nikólaos

Spinalonga Fortress
Spinalonga Island
28410 41773
Daily 9–5.30
Caiques go to Spinalonga Island daily in season from Elounda, every 30 mins 9–4.30
Expensive

HIGHLIGHTS

- The harbour
- Ancient Olous
- Venetian fortress

Head towards the high life at Elounda where hotels bask in self-contained luxury. The town itself is more down to earth, and the adjacent peninsula and island of Spinalonga are of great interest.

Stunning views The road to Elounda from Agios Nikolaos skirts high above the Bay of Mirabello and has stunning views to the rugged Ornos Mountains in the east. Luxury hotels command the coastal heights and several have their own beaches. Elounda itself is centred round a big harbour where fishing boats come and go. Behind it is an equally big town square, a great place to sit watching the always fascinating life of the harbour. The square is lined on its three sides by shops, cafés and restaurants, some of which can be expensive.

Vivid history Just before Elounda proper a road leads over a causeway to the peninsula of Spinalonga, also known as Kolokithia. On the landward side of the peninsula are the vestigial remains of the ancient Graeco-Roman city of Olous. The peninsula has coastal footpaths and is a haven for wildlife. Off the north end of the peninsula is the island of Spinalonga, dominated by its 16th-century Venetian fortress. Not even the Ottoman Empire could subdue it and the fortress only succumbed in 1715, 46 years after the conquest. From 1903 until 1957 the island was a leper colony. Only ruins, and numerous day visitors, inhabit Spinalonga today.

A surviving windmill (left); grazing sheep above the plateau (right)

Lasithiou Plateau

Think Tibet—almost, when you climb the endlessly twisting roads to the Lasithiou Plateau, a broad basin of fertile land that nestles high in the Dikti Mountains above Agios Nikolaos.

Gaunt peaks A world in its own right, the Lasithiou Plateau lies high in the Dikti Mountains surrounded by gaunt peaks. Once famous for its huge number of windmills, the plateau has lost some of its charm as countless tour buses grunt and grumble up the mountain roads to make the circuit of the green expanse. The windmills are not so visually evident these days as mechanical pumps have supplanted them, but once they were essential for irrigation of the fields where corn, potatoes and fruit, such as pears, were grown.

Farming tradition The Venetians established a farming tradition here, but only after they had reduced the plateau to a barren waste for a hundred years, as punishment for rebellion. A series of villages punctuates the circular road, the largest being Tzermiado and Agios Konstantinos. At the village of Agios Georgios there is an appealing little Folk Museum, but the main sight on Lasithiou is the Dikteon Andron (Dikteon Cave) at the southwest corner of the plateau. If you're fit hike the 6km (3.5 miles) up to the ancient site of Karfi, a last stronghold of the Minoans against Mycenaean and Dorian encroachment. The hike starts at Tzermiadho, at the northeast corner of the plateau.

THE BASICS

M4

Southwest of Agios Nikolaos

Taverna Antonis (€), between the villages of Psichro and Plati (tel 28440 31581)

Two a day Mon–Sat from Agios Nikolaos and Iraklio

No access possible to Dikteon Cave, but villages can be visited

Folk Museum

Agios Georgios

Easter–Oct Tue–Sun 9.30–2.30, Tue and Thu 5–8pm

Inexpensive

HIGHLIGHTS

- The plateau
- Dikteon Cave (▷ 98)
- Karfi

Panagia Kera

Panagia Kera church (left); a gilded fresco inside the church (right)

THE BASICS

- N5
- Kritsa, 10km (6 miles) southwest of Agios Nikolaos
- 28410 51806
- Tue–Sun 9–3
- Café on premises (€), Paradise Restaurant across the road (€€)
- Seven a day Mon–Fri from Agios Nikolaos, four Sat–Sun
- Few
- Moderate
- Shop

HIGHLIGHTS

- The Holy Family frescoes
- Herod's banquet fresco
- The Last Supper fresco

TIP

- It may seem obvious, but this popular church is so small that an early or late visit, within opening hours, offers the best chance of contemplating the frescoes unimpeded.

Downsize your expectations as far as the size of this enthralling, but tiny church goes. Inside, however, is a dazzling feast of superb frescoes that reflect the down to earth approach of Crete's Byzantine painters.

Outstanding frescoes At first glance the restored Byzantine Church of Panagia Kera may seem like another restored Greek church surrounded by trees. But step inside and the frescoed walls seem to expand to create a space as big as a cathedral. The frescoes on the walls of the triple naves of the church are some of the finest in Crete and in all of Greece. They represent a transition from the classical fresco painting of the early Byzantine period to the compelling Naturalism of later painters. The church interior can be dark, but with the doors open, the light illuminates the walls.

Story telling The wall paintings of the south aisle show scenes from the life of the Virgin Mary and her mother, St. Anne. It is here that an earthly narrative quality asserts itself in the depiction of a disgruntled Joseph and dejected Mary on their way to Bethlehem, as an angel arrives to counsel Joseph. The north aisle paintings depict scenes of the Last Supper and, down to its left, Herod's banquet with Salome in full dance mode. There are two similar depictions of warrior saints, the first of St. George slaying the dragon, the other of St. Demetrius dispatching a robber.

Spring flowers fringe the beach (left), while palm trees line the promenade (right)

TOP 25

Sitia

It may seem a bit out on a limb as far as the rest of Crete goes, but Sitia, with its wide, generous harbour and splendid promenade, is a true gem and is certainly fit to rub shoulders with Crete's better-known centres.

Rugged mountains Sitia stands in the corner of a beautiful bay, with views to rugged mountains across the Bay of Sitia. It is a working port, but has a strong tourism element, aided by the town being on the ferry route triangle with Iraklio and Santorini and having a small airport. Sitia was recorded as a settlement in the Graeco-Roman period, but finds within the area indicate a previous Minoan settlement and a later Hellenic town. The Venetians built a walled settlement and fortress, the Kazarma, now the site of an open-air theatre whose major event is the Kornaria Festival (mid-Jul to Aug) featuring concerts, stage plays and Cretan dancing.

Destruction Most of Sitia's Venetian buildings were destroyed by earthquakes and by the Muslim pirate Barbarossa. Today, the town has a fresh, modern look and there is a delightful promenade. Sitia's sandy beach stretches east from the town. It can be breezy in the bay, and the area is popular with windsurfers. The town's Archaeological Museum is a little way south of the centre near the bus station. It has some fine exhibits, many from Zakros (▷ 96), but, in pride of place, the exquisite ivory statuette of a young man (*c.* 1450) discovered at Palekastro.

THE BASICS

Q4

70km (43 miles) east of Agios Nikolaos

Kastro (€€)

Regular service from Agios Nikolaos, Iraklio and Ierapetra

Archaeological Museum

Odos Piskokefalou

28430 23917

Tue–Sun 8.30–3

Few

Moderate

HIGHLIGHTS

- The harbourside promenade
- Archaeological Museum
- The Folk Museum

TIP

- A visit to Sitia's Folk Museum reveals interesting traditional artefacts including a weaving loom.

Kapetan Sifinos 28

28430 22861

Mon–Fri 10–1

Zakros Palati

TOP 25

HIGHLIGHTS

- View of the town from the high ground
- Central shrine
- Gorge of the Dead ravine

You have to keep going to reach Zakros. It's worth it, for the drive and for the marvellous location. There's a pebbly beach, a little harbour and a clutch of tavernas to go with some intriguing Minoan ruins.

Thriving centre In Minoan times Zakros was a thriving centre with a harbour that is now well inland. Trade with Egypt and the Middle East says much about the influences and possible cultural connections attached to the Minoan civilization. The Cretan archaeologist Nikolaos Platon uncovered the Palace of Zakros itself in the 1960s. A huge number of Linear A tablets were discovered, and many treasures from the palace are housed in the Archaeological Museums at Iraklio (▷ 24) and Sitia (▷ 95).

Clockwise from far left: Uncovered Minoan remains scattered across the hillside; terrapins make their home beside the well at the Palace of Zakros; dawn rises over the rugged escarpment and Minoan site; ancient vases found at the site

Today, the site may seem fairly small, but it has an absorbing appeal, not least because of its location below red-hued cliffs, its slightly untended appearance and the tantalizing knowledge that it was once accessible by sea.

Royal ruins Zakros dates from the period 1700–1400BC. What you see today are the ruins of royal quarters, a ceremonial hall and banqueting hall, shrines, storerooms, workshops, wells and cisterns. Excavators discovered 3,500-year-old olives preserved in water at the bottom of a jar and are said to have tasted them and found them palatable. In the rocky escarpment behind the site is the entrance to the impressive ravine known as the Gorge of the Dead (Faragi Nekron), so called because of Minoan burial caves in its depths.

THE BASICS

- R5
- Kato Zakros, 45km (28 miles) east of Sitia
- 28430 26897
- Check for times
- Akrogiali (€), Kato Zakros beach (tel 28430 26897)
- Two a day Mon, Tue and Fri from Sitia
- None
- Moderate; free on Sun in winter

More to See

DIKTEON ANDRON

The main sight on the Lasithiou Plateau (▷ 93) is the Dikteon Andron (Dikteon Cave), another contender for being the birthplace of Zeus. The cave is awesome enough to fit the bill certainly, although concrete stairways and modern lighting diminish the full impact of the huge stalactites, stalagmites and organ pipe formations, while once again you will join crowds of fellow visitors in high season.

M5 Psychro, Lasithiou 29770 364335 Apr–Oct daily 8–7; Nov–Mar 8.30–3 Tavernas near by Two a day Mon–Sat from Agios Nikolaos; one a day from Iraklio None Moderate; expensive with guide and if you take a donkey to the entrance Parking is limited. It's a steep walk to the entrance

GOURNIA

This atmospheric and little-visited Minoan-era site, dating from 1600 to 1500BC, was destroyed in 1450 and re-colonized by the Mycaeneans from 1375 to 1200BC. The ruins stand waist-high and give an excellent impression of the density and scale of the originals. At the high point are the ruins of a palace that was three storeys high in its day.

P5 19km (12 miles) southeast of Agios Nikolaos 28410 24943 Tue–Sun 8.30–3 Fish tavernas at nearby Pachia Ammos Regular service to Agios Nikolaos and Sitia None Inexpensive Some finds from Gournia are housed in the Archaeological Museum in Iraklio (▷ 24) and a few in the museum at Sitia (▷ 95)

IERAPETRA

There should be prizes for pronouncing Ierapetra's name (try Ya-*rah*-petra). The most southerly town in Europe, Ierapetra is surrounded by plastic greenhouses, vegetable growing being the main industry of the area. Only when you reach the harbour and the old Venetian fortress do you begin to appreciate the town's rough-cut charm. Behind the harbour is the

Entrance to Dikteon Cave

An Ottoman mosque in Ierapetra's central square

old Turkish quarter, with a mosque and fountain and a pleasing tangle of lanes. The Archaeological Museum is a few streets northwest of the harbour.

N6 35km (22 miles) south of Agios Nikolaos Cafés and tavernas along the waterfront Regular service to Agios Nikolaos, Iraklio and Sitia None

LATO

The post-Minoan, Dorian town (seventh–third century BC) of Lato occupies a marvellous location high in the hills above Agios Nikolaos. Lato has a simpler structure than Crete's Minoan-era sites, but the ruins are extensive. They rise in tiers and are characterized by huge stone blocks that were used for the entrance gateway, the guard towers and workshops, but also for olive presses. The road to the site is through lovely wooded countryside.

N4 3.5km (2 miles) north of Kritsa Tue–Sun 8.30–3 Tavernas in Kritsa Seven a day Mon–Fri, four Sat–Sun, to Kritsa None Moderate

MAKRYGIALOS

One of southeast Crete's best beaches has made Makrygialos and its sister village Analipsi into very pleasant adjoining resorts. The main road slices through town, but the beach and its promenade make up for everything and are served by cafés, bars and tavernas. The sea is shallow and is ideal for families.

Q5 24km (15 miles) east of Ierapetra Tavernas on the seafront Four a day Mon–Sat from Sitia and Ierapetra, two a day Sun None

MALIA

Malia is Crete's liveliest and brashest resort, yet just next door is the outstanding Minoan site, the Palace of Malia. The resort has a long beach and speaks—or shouts happily—for itself with countless bars and clubs ruling the roost. The Palace of Malia is 3km (2 miles) to the east on a peaceful tree-studded plain between the sea and the Dikti Mountains. The ruins are much lower key than those at Knossos.

A temple at the Dorian site of Lato

Malia beach, with an island church offshore

M4 36km (24 miles) east of Iraklio Palace of Malia: 28970 31597 Numerous cafés and restaurants (€–€€€) Regular service from Iraklio and Agios Nikolaos Palace of Malia: Apr–Oct Tue–Sun 8.30–7.30; Nov–Mar Tue–Sun 8.30–3 Palace of Malia: Moderate

MOHLOS

The tiny seaside village of Mohlos, reached down winding roads, is a charming place with some good fish tavernas and upmarket accommodation. Swimming is possible, but the absence of a big beach is something of a plus. The visible remains of a late-Minoan town on an offshore islet lends added kudos. Farther offshore is the larger islet of Psira, also with Minoan remains; local boats will take you there.

P4 40km (25 miles) east of Agios Nikolaos Cafés and tavernas Regular service from Agios Nikolaos and Sitia

MONI TOPLOU

One of Crete's most enterprizing monasteries, Moni Toplou is noted for its produce, including organic olive oil and wine. The 14th-century monastery lies in the empty hills east of Sitia and was fortified to deter pirate attacks. Moni Toplou is now invaded by visitors. The most notable of the many icons in the church is the Lord Thou Art Great (1770), consisting of more than 60 miniature paintings.

R4 16km (10 miles) east of Sitia 28430 61226 Apr–Oct daily 9–6 Café/snack bar (€) From Sitia, then a 3km (1.5 miles) walk from the main road Few Inexpensive

VAI BEACH

Rare date palms add real exotica to Vai beach but also add to its popularity, especially in the high season, when the lovely sands are buried beneath beach lovers. Water sports are a main distraction, too. Plan to go early or late in the day and season.

R4 9km (5.5 miles) north of Palekastro Café and taverna Few buses from Sitia via Palekastro

Moni Toplou, set in fine gardens

Glorious sands at Vai beach

Agios Nikolaos

Agios Nikolaos is not a big place; this short stroll takes you through the heart of the town and along the exhilarating waterfront area.

DISTANCE: 2km (1.5 miles) **ALLOW:** 2 hours

START

THE HARBOUR
N4

1. From the harbour jetty turn right and head along the waterfront road of Akti I Koundourou with the harbour on your left.

2. Where the road bends south, pass a striking harp-like sculpture of metal and glass on a small promontory from where there are magnificent views of the mountains across the bay.

3. Follow the seafront road to reach Kitroplatia Beach with its swathe of cafés and tavernas.

4. At the far end of the beach go left in front of several tavernas and follow the walkway leading round a rocky headland. There are more fine views across the bay, and wayside seats for picnicking.

5. As the walkway ends above the marina keep straight up K. Sfakianiki.

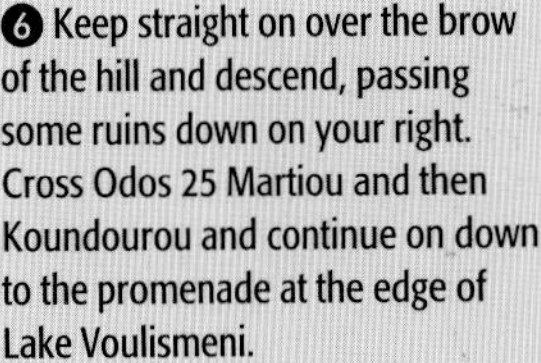

6. Keep straight on over the brow of the hill and descend, passing some ruins down on your right. Cross Odos 25 Martiou and then Koundourou and continue on down to the promenade at the edge of Lake Voulismeni.

7. The lake was once cut off from the sea and a channel was cut through to the sea in 1867. Head right round the lake and walk up Odos Paleologou to visit the Archaeological Museum.

8. Retrace your steps to visit the small folk museum that lies between Lake Voulismeni and the outer harbour. Now relax in one of the lakeside cafés.

THE HARBOUR
N4

END

Lasithiou Plateau

It's uphill all the way to the Lasithiou Plateau, then a circuit of one of Crete's fascinating features, visiting the Dikteon Cave on the way.

DISTANCE: 83km (51 miles) **ALLOW:** 6–7 hours including stops

START

NEAPOLI

N4

❶ Follow the sign for Lasithiou from the main square in Neapoli. The road twists its way scenically up through the mountains through seemingly endless twists and turns. Real driving!

❷ After 26km (16 miles), the plateau opens suddenly below you, a broad green plain ringed by rugged, stony peaks.

❸ At the village of Mesa Lasithiou, turn right at the road junction, by a church, for Tzermiado (signposted to Dzermido and Iraklio).

❹ Signed from the main road, on the way is the Kronio Cave, used as a burial site from prehistoric times. Just before the parking area, there are guides (optional) to show you the way.

❺ At Tzermiado, there are several cafés and tavernas for refreshment.

❻ Continue along the road beyond Tzermiado and at the junction at Pinakiano go straight on, following signs for Psychro.

❼ Beyond the village of Plati, follow signs for the Dikteon Cave (▷ 98). Parking for the cave is limited. Note: parking at the side of the approach road is not advised, as local police are quite strict when it comes to enforcing penalties.

❽ Continue anti-clockwise around the plateau until you reach Agios Georgios. which has a small folk museum, well signed from the centre. At Agios Konstantinos turn off right to return to Neapoli.

NEAPOLI

N4

END

Shopping

BIBLIOPOLEIO
A useful place in Elounda for Greek and foreign newspapers and a selection of foreign language paperbacks.
N4 Platia Eloundas, Elounda 28410 41641

BYZANTO
Hand-painted icon artists explain techniques such as the cracking of the gold leaf to get the antique look. All of them are copies from old churches and monasteries throughout Greece. The icons come signed and with a certificate.
N4 Odos 28 Oktovriou 14, Agios Nikolaos 28410 26530

CERAMICA 1
Nic Gabriel keeps the spirit of traditional Greek forms alive with his handmade copies of ceramics from museums all over Greece. Each piece comes with a certificate of provenance and information about the history of the original. Shipping can be arranged.
N4 Odos Paleologou, Agios Nikolaos 28410 24075

FASHION CONSCIOUS
Agios Nikolaos's reputation for fashion is well supported in Odos 28 Oktovriou, the main street running inland from the harbour. Here you'll find boutiques, jewellery shops and craft galleries.
N4

GEORGIOS EKATERINIDIS
A food shop where you can buy local products, and especially the area's famous honey from bees that feed on thyme and impart an unbeatable flavour.
Q4 Riga Fereou 18, Sitia 28430 28468

KERA
Several doors take you into this treasure house of gifts and souvenirs to satisfy all tastes, from icons to jewellery, fabrics and pottery.
N4 Koundourou, Agios Nikolaos 28410 22292

MARKETS
Weekly markets are a feature of Lasithiou province, especially in the larger centres. There's an excellent market selling produce and other goods in Agios Nikolaos on a Wednesday morning, and a similar market on Saturday mornings in Ierapetra.

OIL OF THE GODS

Crete, and not least the Sitia region, is noted for its excellent olive oil, over 90 per cent of which is classified as extra virgin, the product of cold pressing without further processing. Its acidity does not rise above 0.7 per cent. Many claims for enhancing health and longevity are made on behalf of olive oil, and history underpins this. The ancient Greeks used oil in food but also for such things as treatment for burns and as body lotion.

MONI TOPLOU
Organic growing is the rule here, and in the monastery shop you can buy splendid wines from organically grown grapes such as Laitiko, as well as raki, high quality extra-virgin olive oil and delicious honey from thyme-fed bees.
R4 6km (10 miles) east of Sitia 28430 61226
Apr–Oct daily 9–6

PETRAKIS ICON WORKSHOP
Looking for an icon? Try this gallery in Elounda where painted icons using traditional materials and methods are created. Sculptures, pottery and jewellery are also for sale.
N4 Odos A. Papandreou 22, Elounda 28410 41669

WINE CO-OPERATIVE OF SITIA
The co-operative represents over 8,000 farmers in the region, and as well as selling farming equipment and supplies it sells excellent local wines and olive oil of the finest quality. The co-operative is on the road into Sitia from the west.
Q4 Missonos 74, Sitia 28430 22211

Entertainment and Activities

ARMIDA

Join the pirates in Agios Nikolaos' outer harbour, where this old wooden vessel moors just offshore during the summer. A very different venue from the norm for an evening of cocktails.

N4 ✉ Agios Nikolaos harbour ☎ 69479 92577

BABEL

This harbour-area bar is hugely popular, and open all day and into the early hours when the music cranks up. It has a large screen TV for big sports fixtures and the internet for customer use.

N4 ✉ Akti Vritomartidos, Elounda ☎ 28410 42336

DANCE CLUBS

Agios Nikolaos' late-night clubs are clustered around the start of Odos 25 Martiou with names such as Lotus and Passion, where visiting Djs wind up the decibel levels on summer nights.

DIROS BEACH WATERSPORTS

www.spinalonga-windsurf.com

Elounda is known for its great windsurfing conditions, and this beach-based outfit opposite Spinalonga Island caters for beginners to experienced surfers and offers lessons and gear hire. They also rent pedaloes, canoes, banana boats and motor boats.

N4 ✉ Diros Beach Hotel, Elounda ☎ 69449 32760

HAPPY DIVERS

www.happydivers.gr

For all scuba-diving options try this well-run company that offers everything from snorkelling for about €20 to a full Divemaster's course at €700. There is also a range of reasonably priced boat-diving trips and specialist's courses, including underwater photography and night diving.

N4 ✉ Hermes Hotel beach, Agios Nikolaos ☎ 28410 82546

THE LATO

Agios Nikolaos' summer culture-fest sees a colourful programme of theatre, music and dance staged at various venues throughout the town. The tourist office has details of events.

☎ Agios Nikolaos Tourist Information Office: 28410 22357

SUN SAFETY

Boat trips, beach trips, road-train trips and even short-term visits to sights and attractions all mean major sun exposure on Crete, just about any time of the year. There are general warnings enough, but you should always make sure that your skin is covered with applications of high-protection sun cream several times a day, and wear a sun hat that has thick material.

LITTLE TRAIN TOURS

Fun for all the family on a road train that includes trips to the Panagia Kera (▷ 94) as well as shorter trips around Agios Nikolaos. You can pick up the road train from the southeast side of the harbour.

N4 ✉ Themistokleous 12, Agios Nikolaos ☎ 28410 25420

MOLO

This ultra-modern café–bar, on the terrace above the eastern side of the harbour, is the nighttime haunt for Agios Nikolaos' fashion conscious. Great cocktails and drinks go well with House music and Greek sounds into the early hours. It's also ideal for coffee and snacks by day.

N4 ✉ Koundourou 6, Agios Nikolaos ☎ 28410 26250 🕓 Daily 8am–5am

NOSTOS BOAT TRIPS

There are midday departures from Agios Nikolaos harbour on board the *Venus* for a four-hour trip to Spinalonga Island and to the ancient site of Oulus on Spinalonga Peninsula. The trip benefits from having an English-speaking archaeological guide. Nostos Tours also organizes other cruises, fishing trips and night trips.

N4 ✉ Rousou Koundourou Str 30, Agios Nikolaos ☎ 28410 22819

Restaurants

PRICES

Prices are approximate, based on a 3-course meal for one person.

€€€ over €25
€€ €15–€25
€ under €15

DU LAC (€€–€€€)
Long established and popular, the Du Lac has an excellent menu of fish and seafood dishes, plus well-prepared Cretan specialities. It overlooks Agios Nikolaos' Lake Voulismeni, the sea water lagoon at the heart of town.
N4 Omirou, Agios Nikolaos 28410 23783 Daily lunch and dinner

FERRYMAN (€€)
A well-known waterside restaurant that takes its name from the old BBC television series, *Who Pays the Ferryman?* that was filmed at nearby locations. Traditional Cretan food with some international touches enhances the experience.
N4 Elounda waterfront 28410 41230 Daily lunch and dinner

ILIOS CAFÉ (€)
In a great position right above the beach at Makrygialos, this bright, stylish little café offers sandwiches and snacks and is a great place for evening drinks too.
Q5 Makrygialos 28430 51280 All day

LEVANTE (€€)
Down on the Ierapetra harbourfront, this is one of the best of a long line of quayside places. It's always reliable for great fish dishes such as fresh sardines, but also pastitsio pasta layered with minced beef onions and cheese.
N/P6 Samouil 38, Ieraptera 28420 80585 Daily lunch and dinner

MESOSTRATI (€–€€)
Mesostrati is an unpretentious place where the emphasis is on good Cretan food without frills. Local cheese *saganaki* in filo pastry with peppers, tomatoes and herbs is a great starter, and fish dishes are always well prepared.
P4 Mohlos 28430 94170 Daily 10am–late

WINE WINNERS

Eastern Crete is certainly noted for its excellent olive oil, but wine making in the area, as in the rest of Crete, was not considered to have developed as well as it might when compared with Greece's mainland wine producing areas. But wine production has advanced hugely in recent years, not least because growers have stayed with indigenous grape varieties such as Kotsifali and Mandilaria wine, while the Sitia area favours the Liatiko grape.

PELAGOS (€€–€€€)
A certain cachet clings to this fine taverna, not least because of its location in a handsome neoclassical building with a large courtyard shaded by palms. The emphasis is on fish and seafood, with specialities such as mussel *saganaki,* and red mullet with herbs. They also do Cretan-influenced meat and pasta dishes.
N4 Odos Katehak 10, Agios Nikolaos 28410 25737

REMEZZO (€–€€)
Taverans crowd the Sitia waterfront, and the family-run Remezzo is one of the best. They dish up great Cretan favourites as well as mixed-fish plates for two and also vegetarian plates. The wine list has some excellent local vintages.
Q4 El Venizelou 167, Sitia 28430 28607 Daily lunch and dinner

ZYGOS (€–€€)
On the sunny morning side of Lake Voulismeni, this café–restaurant has open views across the lake and the town beyond. It's ideal for morning coffee in the sun, or for tasty offerings such as octopus in olive oil or a seafood platter for two.
N4 E Antistaseos 1, Agios Nikolaos 28410 82009 Daily lunch and dinner

Crete can offer an enormous number of hotel options, from basic resort rooms to luxury hotels with beach access, plus countless self-catering studios, apartments and villas.

Introduction

Many visitors stay in pre-booked resort hotels scattered around Crete but independent travel is increasing, with travellers shopping around for accommodation on arrival. Many resort hotels close in the winter, but in cities and towns and the larger resorts you will usually find a room. At resorts such as Matala (▷ 82) and Elounda (▷ 92) very little is available off-season.

Best Deals

In towns and cities, during summer and at holiday weekends, rooms under €60 are rare. Easter and August are the busiest and most expensive periods when you will pay the full rate. You may have difficulty finding a room if you do not book ahead, although something usually turns up (but often in a take it or leave it way). The best deals are had early and late in the year when hoteliers and room owners often discount prices substantially because they may have several empty rooms. In rural areas you will normally pay less.

Expectations

Many studio rooms and apartments within the budget and mid-range price bands can be exceptional, although there are still plenty of tired-looking rooms throughout Crete that are priced far above their promise. Some resort hotels can have boring rooms and cramped balconies, while 'sea views' usually mean rooms at the front only. Do not be shy of first taking a look at the room and of declining politely. Most mid-range and luxury hotels include a buffet breakfast in the price as do budget hotels.

Take your pick, from waterfront tavernas and hotel villages in landscaped grounds to luxury beachfront hotels

ONLINE BOOKINGS

- Many hotels and apartments have their own websites and they are worth checking out if you plan to book ahead, although they will always cast themselves in the best light. Good sites include www.booking.com, www.laterooms.com, www.expedia.com and www.lastminute.com. For self-catering try www.holiday-rentals.co.uk.

Budget Hotels

PRICES

Expect to pay under €70 per night for a double room in a budget hotel.

ATELIER

www.frosso-bora.com

Tucked away below the walls of the Fortezza, this handful of rooms is above the owner's little pottery (▷ 63). They are immaculate and have cooking facilities.

G3 Himaras 27, Rethymno 28310 24440

GABI'S ROOMS

Gabi's rooms are spacious and immaculate, and lie within a well-tended complex on the seafront with uninterrupted sea views—except for some well-tended tamarisk trees. There are tea and coffee-making facilities in each room.

C4 Sougia 28230 51561/69460 36395

HARIS STUDIOS

www.paleochora-holidays.com

These simple, clean rooms and studios, with cooking facilities, are in a great position at the quiet eastern end of Palaiochora's seafront.

C4 Palaiochora 28320 42438

HAVANIA APARTMENTS

www.havania.com

About 2.5km (1.5 miles) from the centre of Agios Nikolaos, this seafront place has a swimming pool and little private jetty. Family-run, the immaculate studios with cooking facilities are for two and four people.

N4 Agios Nikolaos 28410 28758/82458 Easter–Oct

HOTEL CRETA

This very pleasant hotel has comfortable studio rooms, all with separate kitchenettes. Right at the heart of Agios Nikolaos's waterfront, yet it is on the high ground making it a quiet retreat with terrific views across the Gulf Of Mirabello from the upper floors.

N4 Sarolidi 22, Agios Nikolaos 28410 28893

HOTEL LENA

www.lena-hotel.gr

Tucked away in a quiet little side street, the Lena is a small hotel with immaculate, though sometimes smallish, rooms and friendly family proprietors. A bargain for central Iraklio.

d2 Lahana 10, Iraklio 28102 23280

CHECKING IN

On arrival you will probably be asked for your passport by hotel reception or by room owners. This is to ensure a guarantee of payment, and staff should simply record the necessary details there and then. You should wait for this to be done and for your passport to be returned to you, rather than collecting it later. Recommended hotel and room owners in this guide are to be entirely trusted, but it is better to keep a check on your passport at all times.

KASTRO

www.kastro-hotel.com

Don't expect a scenic outlook at this otherwise decent modern hotel. It's conveniently located in a quiet back street, close to both the town centre and the port.

d2 Theotokopoulou 22, Iraklio 28102 85020

MAKRI STENO

www.makristeno.gr

Firmly at the budget end of the market, this rambling old Venetian house has some very individual, if basic, rooms scattered around its snakes-and-ladders' stairways and terraces. All have cooking facilities.

G3 N. Foka 54–58, Rethymno 28310 55464

MINOS HOTEL

www.minos.agiagalini.com

At the entrance to Agia Galini is this very friendly family-run hotel that has magnificent sea views from the front rooms. All rooms are spotless and well equipped, and there's a useful communal kitchen.

H5 Agia Galini 28320 91292

Mid-Range Hotels

PRICES

Expect to pay between €70 and €130 per night for a double room in a mid-range hotel.

AKTI OLOUS

www.eloundaaktiolous.gr

Overlooking the bay at the entrance to Elounda, this hotel has been renovated to offer comfortable rooms with colourful decor. Most rooms have sea views, and there's a rooftop swimming pool and a small beach.

N4 Elounda 28410 41270 May to mid-Oct

ATRION HOTEL

www.atrion.gr

Fully refurbished to immaculate standards, the Atrion offers friendly and efficient service. Don't expect a scenic location, but the high quality makes up for it.

d2 Odos Chronaki 9, Iraklio 28102 4600

DOGE APARTMENTS

www.dogehotel.com

This old Venetian house near Chania's Venetian harbour has been converted into eight fully equipped apartments.

D2 Odos Kondilaki 14–16, Chania 28210 95466

HALEPA

www.halepa.com

A handsome 19th-century neo-classical building in its own grounds and complete with curving exterior staircase. The Halepa was formerly used as the British Embassy in Chania. Rooms are spacious and have a period style.

D2 El. Venizelos 164, Chania 28210 28440

HOTEL HERMES

A modern hotel that has been pleasantly renovated in recent years, the Hermes is located on the seafront road about 300m (327 yards) from Agios Nikolaos harbour. It has a rooftop swimming pool and roofgarden.

N4 Akti Koundourou, Agios Nikolaos 28410 28253 Apr–Oct

MILIA

If you're looking for a thoroughly 'green' experience, then the unique Milia settlement is the place. Tucked away in the mountains midway between Kissamos and Palaiochora (▷ 52), this once abandoned village has been turned into a complex of eco cottages that are lit by oil lamps and depends on solar panels for electricity with log fires in winter. The complex stands in a deeply wooded valley and all food is organic, much of it coming from Milia's own farm and from the surrounding countryside. Milia can be reached by car on surfaced roads and a final dirt track. Phone to enquire about possible pick up from bus stops.

B3 Vlatos, 50km (31 miles) southwest of Chania 28210 46774/51569; www.milia.gr

HOTEL IDEON

www.hotelideon.gr

Rooms, suites and studios are all of good standard at this seafront hotel near Rethymno's Venetian harbour. It has a swimming pool and a restaurant, and the rooms at the front have great views and generous private balconies.

G3 N. Plastira Square 10, Rethymno 28310 28667–9 Easter–Oct

HOTEL MARINA

www.marinahotelanogia.gr

Hotel Marina has a terrific outlook down across the mountain valley below Anogia. The hotel is only a few years old, and has lovely decor and good facilities. Off season when things can get cold in the high mountains, there are fires and radiators. Located on the north edge of the village.

J4 Anogia 28340 31817

HOTEL PORTO LOUTRO

www.hotelportoloutro.com

Travel on foot or by boat will get you to Loutro and this pleasant hotel. There are separate establishments, Loutro I overlooking the beach, and Loutro II higher up

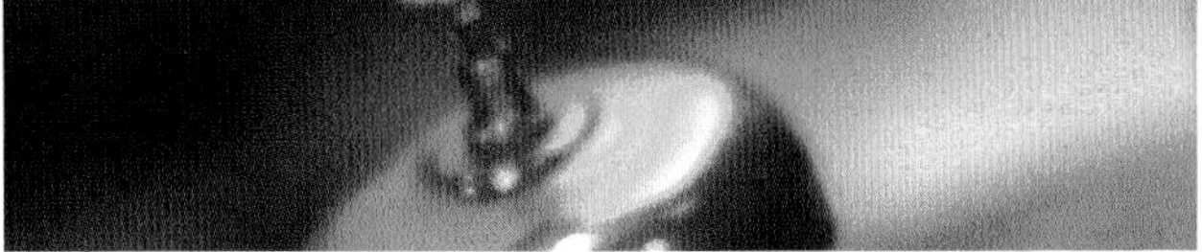

the slopes. A daily boat from Chora Sfakion and Agia Roumeli runs to Loutro daily.
E4 Loutro 28250 91433 Mid-Mar to Oct

MARIN DREAM HOTEL
www.marinhotel.gr
Great views from the higher seafront rooms at this modern hotel encompass Iraklio's harbour and Venetian fortress. Stylish rooms and a roof garden restaurant.
f2 Doukos Bofor 12, Iraklio 28103 00019

NOSTOS
www.nostos-hotel.com
Wooden floors and roofs, exposed brick and stonework enhance the lovely mezzanine rooms and self-catering studios in this very old Venetian house, which has been renovated with style. Some rooms have sea views from the balconies.
D2 Zambeliou 42–46, Chania 28210 94743

OLYMPIC
www.hotelolympic.com
This established Iraklio hotel overlooking the famous Bembo Fountain in Platia Kornarou has had a face-lift in recent years to provide comfortable modern rooms.
d3 Platia Kornarou, Iraklio 28102 88861

PALAZZO
www.palazzohotel.gr
A small cosy hotel in the heart of Chania's old town, Palazzo mixes traditional style and much exposed polished wood with modern amenities and comfort.
D2 54 Theotokopoulou, Chania 22810 93227

PALAZZO VECCHIO
www.palazzovecchio.gr
This boutique hotel is in a quiet area near the sea and just south of the Fortezza. It's a genuine Venetian *palazzo* that has been very well restored. The stylish rooms have retained beamed ceilings and are attractively decorated, and there's a cobbled courtyard and swimming pool.
G3 Corner of Iroon Politechniou and Melissinou, Rethymno 28310 35351

START THE DAY

Most hotels in the mid-range bracket and all in the luxury range include breakfast in their price. Buffet breakfasts either have a basic selection of cereal, cold meat, cheese and eggs with all the trimmings or hot trays of bacon, sausages or scrambled eggs to accompany them. Coffee and tea are always on tap. Luxury hotels offer a huge range of breakfast trimmings. You are unlikely to sample the 'full English' breakfast in Greek run hotels, but many resort cafés rise to the fry-up occasion with relish.

PENSION THEREZA
At the lower end of the range for the price sector, this creaky old Venetian building, on the west side of Chania's Venetian harbour, demands something of a quirky attitude to life. But if you want an authentic sense of the antique, this is for you. There's an upstairs balcony, with communal kitchen and unsurpassed harbour views.
D2 Angelou 8, Chania 28210 92798

SITIA BAY HOTEL
www.sitiabay.com
Only a few years old and in a good location behind Sitia town beach, these fully equipped studios and apartments have the benefit of a swimming pool and a peaceful communal roof terrace.
Q4 Tritis Septemvriou 8, Sitia 28430 24800

STUDIOS YIORGIS
www.paleochora-holidays.com
These lovely studios and rooms are at the lower end of this price band and are of outstanding value; immaculate and spacious, all have cooking facilities. Opened in 2009, the studios are one block back from Palaiochora's western seafront, and there's also a lovely swimming pool out front and a small garden at the rear.
C4 Palaiochora 28230 42438

Luxury Hotels

PRICES

Expect to pay more than €130 per night for a standard double room in a luxury hotel.

CASA DELFINO

www.casadelfino.com

At the heart of old Chania, Casa Delfino is classic 17th-century Venetian style. Its rooms, suites and apartments all have superb individual decor, with much use of marble and polished wood. The Venetian legacy is also mirrored in the Italian Aldo Morelato furnishings.

D2 Theofanous 9, Chania 28210 87400

CASA MOAZZO

www.casamoazzo.gr

Opened in 2009 as an addition to Rethymno's select group of converted Venetian mansions, the charming Casa Moazzo lies close to Rethymno's cathedral. The hotel boasts spacious, high-ceilinged suites with a lavish Greek take on their handsome decor and furnishings.

G3 Tombazi 57, Rethymno 28310 36235

ELOUNDA BEACH HOTEL

www.eloundabeach.gr

Hugely exclusive, the Elounda Beach offers luxurious rooms, bungalows and suites all with bay or garden views. You rub shoulders—at least with the memory—of such past guests as presidents and major celebrities. Watersports centre, floodlit tennis courts, extensive gardens, exclusive beaches and even a heli-pad.

N4 Elounda (2km/1 mile south of Elounda centre) 28410 63000

ISTRON BAY HOTEL

www.istronbay.gr

About 13km (8 miles) east of Agios Nikolaos and overlooking a lovely bay, seclusion, luxury and style are the hallmarks of this fine hotel. Decor has Cretan flair, and rooms range from standard and superior to apartments and suites. Facilities include a pool, tennis court, beach bar, watersports, fishing trips and organized activities.

N4 Istron, Agios Nikolaos 28410 61303

VENETIAN VIEW

Many hotels and pensions, in Rethymno and Chania especially, are located in historic houses of the Venetian period that have been overlaid with Ottoman features. In the luxury sector they have been modernized without compromising style. In smaller pensions, full modernization may not always have taken place and there can be a certain antique patina to the decor and furnishings that is still very enjoyable and is certainly not bland.

LATO

www.lato.gr

A stylish, well-equipped hotel, close to the old port, the Lato caters for both business and leisure visitors. Modern, soundproofed guest rooms have all facilities, and many have stunning views of the Venetian fortress and beyond. The hotel's Brillant and Herb's Garden restaurants (▷ 36) are highly recommended.

e2 Epimenidou 15, Iraklio 28102 28103

MOHLOS VILLAS

www.mohlos.com

This complex of just three delightful villas stands on high ground above the seaside village of Mohlos. Cobbled drives and walkways lined with trees and shrubs add to the seclusion, and each villa has its own swimming pool.

N4 Mohlos, 27km (17 miles) east of Agios Nikolaos 28430 94616

VENETO

www.veneto.gr

In the same old Venetian building as the restaurant (▷ 68) of the same name, the hotel's labyrinth of exposed walls, archways and rambling staircases create a haven of peace and individuality. Studios and suites have cooking facilities.

G3 Epimenidou 4, Rethymno 28310 56634

Need to Know

A visit to Crete will be an enjoyable and straightforward experience. Some aspects of Cretan life might seem strange at first, but it's best to celebrate the differences and go with the flow.

Planning Ahead

When to Go

Good times to visit Crete are April until late June, and September until mid-October, when it's not too hot and there are fewer visitors. Late June, July and August are the busiest and hottest times. Winter can see rain on the coast and snow in the mountains, but also glorious spring-like days.

TIME

Crete is two hours ahead of Britain, seven hours ahead of New York, 10 hours ahead of Los Angeles.

AVERAGE DAILY MAXIMUM TEMPERATURES

JAN	FEB	MAR	APR	MAY	JUN	JUL	AUG	SEP	OCT	NOV	DEC
55°F	59°F	61°F	64°F	74°F	82°F	86°F	88°F	79°F	75°F	66°F	61°F
13°C	15°C	16°C	18°C	23°C	28°C	30-°C	31°C	26°C	24°C	19°C	14°C

Spring (March to May) is generally mild but with occasional bouts of very cold and wet weather in the mountains. The south coast is the warmest.

Summer (June to mid-September) becomes increasingly hot with days of unbroken sunshine.

Autumn (mid-September to November), while the sea temperature can be at its highest, there is a chance of rain in the mountains.

Winter (December to February) is a mix of dull wet weather and fresh, sunny days. Snow falls in the mountains and occasionally there has been short-lived snow on low ground.

WHAT'S ON

January–February *Pre-Lenten:* carnival season with the biggest event in Rethymno.
Kathari Deftera: Clean Monday, the Monday before Ash Wednesday; picnics and kite flying.

March *Independence Day* (25 Mar): parades and folk dancing to celebrate the beginning of the revolt against Turkish rule in 1821.

April *Easter* (moveable): a major event in the Greek religious calendar.
Battle of Crete (end of May): celebrations in Chania.

June *Summer Solstice and St. John the Baptist* (24 Jun): with midsummer bonfires.

July *Rethymno's Renaissance Festival.*
Chania's Summer Festival, Iraklio Summer Festival and Agios Nikolaos Lato Festival (Jul–Aug): all with music, dance, theatre and arts events.
Cretan Wine Festival (mid-Jul): in Rethymno.

August *Sultana Festival* (mid-Aug): in Sitia.
Feast of the Assumption (15 Aug).
Palaiochora Music Festival (late Aug–Sep).
Feast of Agios Titos (25 Aug): patron saint of Crete.

October *Chestnut Festival:* in southwest villages, especially Elos.
Ohi Day (No Day): celebrates refusal by Prime Minister Ioannis Metaxas of Mussolini's request to march Italian troops through Greece in 1940.

November Commemoration in Rethymno and Arkadi of explosion at Arkadi Monastery in 1866 (7–9 Nov).

December *St. Nicholas Day* (6 Dec): celebration of the saint, especially at Agios Nikolaos.

Crete Online

www.infocrete.com
Excellent quick index that links to scores of local websites and includes town and village sites, tavernas, hotels, rooms, activities and much more.

www.cretetravel.com
An excellent general site covering every aspect of life and travel in Crete with good updating, news, blogs and links.

www.explorecrete.com
This good overall guide to the island has extensive descriptions of sights and attractions and useful information on beaches, activities and practicalities.

www.crete.tournet.gr
Covers most holiday needs and information and has a useful map section navigating ancient sites and other attractions.

www.interkriti.org
A very busy site with a huge amount of information on everything you need to know, with links to accommodation, car rental and local agents.

www.livingcrete.net
Aimed at those living in Crete but with much insider information that holidaymakers might find useful, even for holidaymakers.

www.cretegazette.com
Website version of a free news and features magazine to keep you up to date on aspects of Cretan life.

www.culture.gr
The official portal of the Hellenic Ministry of Culture, with information about museums and archaeological sites.

USEFUL TRAVEL SITES

www.greeka.com
A general Greece guide that has good travel information, accommodation and useful links.

www.gtp.gr
Web equivalent of the major travel 'bible', Greek Travel Pages, with ferry and air-travel information and accommodation options.

INTERNET CAFÉS

Internet
A friendly spot with good internet access.
✉ Handakos 30, Iraklio
☎ 28103 46168 🕒 Early 'til late 💶 €1.20 per hour

Triple W
Well-equipped internet and gaming centre. Also does printing and scanning.
✉ Valintinou 1, Chania
☎ 28210 93478 🕒 Daily 24 hours 💶 €2 per hour

Cybernet
Long established 24-hour internet centre.
✉ Kalergi 44, Rethymno
☎ 28311 00140 🕒 Daily 24 hours 💶 €2 per hour

Internet station in the Tourism Information Centre
✉ Akti I Koundourou 20, Agios Nikolaos ☎ 28410 22357 🕒 Daily 8.30–9.30 💶 €2 per half hour

Getting There

ENTRY REQUIREMENTS

For the latest passport and visa information check the UK Foreign Office website at www.fco.gov.uk, or the US Department of State at www.state.gov

TOURIST INFORMATION

Iraklio
✉ Xanthoudidi 1
☎ 28102 46299
🕐 Daily Apr–Oct 8.30–8.30; Nov–Mar 8.30–3

Rethymno
✉ Delfini Building, Eleftheriou Venizelou
☎ 28310 29148
🕐 Apr–Oct daily 9–6, Sat 9–4

Chania
✉ M. Mylonogianni
☎ 28210 36155
🕐 Daily 8–2.30

Agios Nikolaos
✉ Akti I Koundourou 20
☎ 28410 22357
🕐 Daily 8.30–9.30

Sitia
✉ K. Karamanli
☎ 28430 28300
🕐 Mon–Fri 9–2.30, 5–8.30

AIRPORTS

Crete is easily reached from international destinations, mainly through Athens, although there are direct flights from European countries during peak times. International and domestic airports are at Iraklio and Chania, while Sitia airport only handles limited domestic destinations.

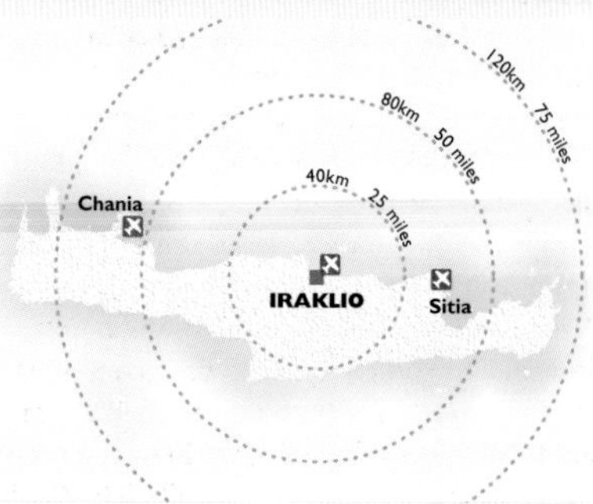

FROM IRAKLIO

Nikos Kazantzakis International Airport, 4km (2.5 miles) east of city centre (☎ 28102 29191), is busy all year and can be very crowded during peak times in July and August. Aegean Airlines (☎ 28103 30475/44324; www.aegeanair.com) and Olympic Air (☎ 28102 44802; www.olympicair.com) operate daily domestic flights to and from Athens and Thessaloniki, and several flights a week to other Greek destinations. Most of the latter involve a flight change at Athens. Aegean Airlines operates some direct flights to European destinations. Sky Express (☎ 28102 23500; www.skyexpress.gr) operates direct flights to internal destinations. Easyjet (www.easyjet.com) operates direct flights from British airports to Iraklio and Chania from about mid-April to October. From about Easter to October numerous charter flights arrive at Iraklio Airport. The Arrivals Hall has an information desk (☎ 28103 97129), airline company desks, car hire outlets, internet, cash machines and a snack bar. There is a left-luggage facility outside the airport building. Local bus No. 1

runs between the airport and Iraklio's Platia Eleftherias about every 15 minutes from 6am to 1am (€0.90). Tickets are from a machine. A taxi costs about €12.

FROM CHANIA

K. Daskalogiannis (Souda Airport), 15km (9 miles) northeast of Chania (☎ 28210 83800), has daily flights to Athens and Thessaloniki operated by Aegean Airlines (☎ 28210 63366; www.aegeanair.com) and Olympic Airlines (☎ 28210 63264; www.olympicairlines.com). Regular charter flights arrive at Chania Airport from about May to October. The Arrivals Hall has an information desk, airline company desks, car-hire outlets and cash machines. There is no left-luggage facility. Buses run from Chania Bus Station to the airport about three times daily (€2.60). A taxi costs about €20.

FROM SITIA

Sitia Airport, 1km (0.5 miles) west of Sitia (☎ 28430 24424), has several flights a week to Athens and to Iraklio. There are few facilities at the airport and no public transport. A taxi costs about €6.

ARRIVING BY SEA

Crete's main ferry ports are all on the north coast. They are Iraklio, Chania, Rethymno, Agios Nikolaos and Sitia. There are daily connections to Piraeus from Iraklio, Rethymno and Chania, and two connections a week from Agios Nikolaos and Sitia. There are several connections a week from all of these ports to several of the Cycladic Islands, including Santorini and Mykonos, and also to Rhodes. There are several connections from Kissamos, in the west of Crete, to Gythio in the Peloponnese and to the island of Kythira. A single ticket economy class from Piraeus to Iraklio is about €36. The trip takes about 6–8 hours. The cost of bringing a car to Crete from Piraeus is about €90. (See panel for ferry operators.)

INSURANCE

Check your insurance policy and buy any necessary supplements. EU nationals receive reduced emergency medical treatment with the relevant documentation (EHIC card for Britons) but full travel insurance is advised and is essential for other visitors.

CUSTOMS

Provided it is for personal use, EU nationals can bring back as much as they like, although you should be aware of add-on costs for baggage operated by some airlines. Current guidelines are: 800 cigarettes, 200 cigars, 1kg tobacco, 10 litres spirits, 20 litres of aperitifs, 90 litres of wine. Some anti-terror restrictions on liquids and sharp instruments in cabin luggage are still current.

FERRY OPERATORS

Blue Star Ferries ☎ 21089 19820; www.bluestarferries.com
ANEK Lines ☎ 28102 44912; www.anek.gr
GA Ferries ☎ 28102 22408; www.gaferries.gr
LANE Lines ☎ 28103 46440; www.lane.gr
Minoan Lines ☎ 28102 29624; www.minoan.gr
Useful ferry information websites are: www.openseas.gr or www.gtp.gr

Getting Around

VISITORS WITH A DISABILITY

Greece is beginning to improve access for those with mobility problems and several hotels and sights, such as museums, have good access. However, the very appeal of the island's numerous ancient sites and old buildings, streets and villages rests on their many flights of steps and often cobbled surfaces. Modern resorts can be more amenable, although even here pavements are sometimes rare and ramps non-existent. For useful information check the website of the Royal Association for Disability and Rehabilitation, RADAR (✉ 12 City Forum, 250 City Road, London EC1V 8AF ☎ 0171 250 3222; www.radar.org.uk).

STUDENTS AND SENIOR CITIZENS

An International Student Identity Card (ISIC) can provide reductions in entrance prices to museums and historic sites. Senior Citizens enjoy reduced rates for the same.

Crete has an excellent local bus network. Boat services ply between the more remote villages on the southwest coast, and there are numerous car and scooter rental outlets at airports, cites and resorts. Always check the car or bike in front of rental personnel before driving off.

BUSES

Services are operated by KTEL, a consortium of several companies. This results in some disparities and confusion, but by and large the system is excellent and timetables are generally adhered to. Main bus stations have current printed timetables. Internet information can be obtained on: www.bus-service-crete-ktel.com or www.cretetravel.com.

BUS STATIONS

Iraklio has two bus stations. Bus Station A (✉ Leoforos Nearchou ☎ 28102 46534) is located on the seafront road in front of the Megaron Hotel. Buses run east to Rethymno and Chania from here, and to all destinations to the east and southeast. Bus No. 2 runs to Knossos from an adjoining stop in Bus Station A. A more central Knossos bus stop is on the west side of Platia Eleftherias. Bus Station B (✉ 9 Machis Kritis ☎ 28102 55965) is located about a kilometre west of Platia Venizelou. Buses for the west and southwest operate from here. Numbered city buses operate within Iraklio city limits, and for visitors, most places of interest are within walking distance of the centre.

Rethymno's bus station (✉ Igoumenou Gavril ☎ 28310 22212) is on the west side of town, overlooking the sea. It has a left-luggage facility and snack bar.

Chania's bus station (✉ Kydonias 73–77 ☎ 28210 93052) is about half a kilometre south of the Venetian Harbour. It has a left-luggage facility and snack bar.

DRIVING

Driving in Crete is on the right-hand side of the road. The island's main road network is

good although it does not always have the precise road markings of other countries. Rural roads can be very narrow and can have some axle-crunching potholes, so drive slowly and be alert–if using a hire car it is not advised to drive on unsurfaced roads and tracks. Mountain roads often have spectacular multiple hairpins. The use of seat belts is compulsory, and children under ten should not ride in a front seat. Drink driving is a very serious offence in Greece and random checks by police are increasing; a blood alcohol level of 0.05 brings an instant fine; over 0.09 is a criminal offence for which you may be jailed. The speed limit is 100kph (62mph) on main highways, 90kph (56mph) on lesser main roads and 50kph (31mph) in built-up areas. Always carry your driving licence.

GUIDED TOURS

There are numerous coach trips to various places throughout the island. Book through travel agents, hotels or bus station offices.

MAPS

You will be deluged with maps dished out by tourism offices, hotels, car-hire companies and even restaurants. Some can be useful, especially the city maps supplied by tourism offices. For comprehensive maps of all of Crete try Road Editions (✉ Handakos 29, Iraklio ☎ 28103 44610) or Planet International Bookshop (✉ Handakos 73, Iraklio ☎ 28102 89605).

TAXIS

Taxis are a reasonable option in Crete, but always ascertain the price beforehand. Luggage is usually surcharged, but blatantly inflated charges should be questioned. If you are not satisfied, phone the Tourist Police. Iraklio has main taxi stands at Bus Station A and in Platia Eleftherias (☎ 28102 10102). Rethymno's main taxi stands are in Platia Martiron and at the north end of Eleftheriou Venizelou (☎ 28310 25000). In Chania you will find the main taxi stand in Platia 1866 (☎ 28210 98700).

WALK WARILY

Roads and streets in Crete do not always have clear-cut pavements or pedestrian walkways. Be careful when walking along traffic-heavy streets. In Iraklio especially, faded road markings at pedestrian crossings indicate a general easygoing attitude to the pedestrian's right of way. Cross with care anywhere. Road works are not always marked off or protected. When walking in towns and villages at night, keep an eye open for unguarded holes and depressions in pavements, and for sudden step-downs in pavements.

DRIVING TIPS

Local drivers may push to overtake, regardless of being on a main road or a narrow lane. It is often best to slow down and pull in, when you can–do not pull off abruptly onto a lay-by as there is often a sharp drop at the edge of the road. When meeting another vehicle at a constricted section of road, if the opposing driver flashes their headlights it means that they are about to proceed. If a village street is becoming ever more narrow, back off before it becomes a donkey track.

Essential Facts

EMERGENCY NUMBERS

- Police 100
- Fire 199
- Forest Fire 191
- Ambulance 166

MONEY

The euro (€) is the official currency of Greece. Notes are in denominations of 5, 10, 20, 50, 100, 200 and 500 euros, and coins are in denominations of 1, 2, 5, 10, 20, 50 cents and 1 and 2 euros.

Cities and main towns, and an increasing number of resorts and larger villages, have ATMs. Credit cards are widely accepted in shops and in some restaurants, but cash is still very much a part of Cretan life, so it is wise to have cash with you especially in resorts.

5 euros

10 euros

50 euros

100 euros

CONSULATES

- Australia ☎ 210 645 0404 (Athens)
- Canada/USA ☎ 210 721 2951 (Athens)
- France ✉ Odos Kritovoulidou 22, Iraklion ☎ 28102 85618; ✉ Odos Manousogiannakidon 32, Chania ☎ 28102 85618
- Germany ✉ Odos Dikaiosynis 7, Iraklio ☎ 28102 26288
- Ireland ✉ Odos Knossou 278, Iraklio ☎ 28102 15060
- Italy ✉ Odos Zografou 13, Iraklio ☎ 28103 42561; ✉ Odos Tzanakaki 70, Chania ☎ 28210 27315
- UK ✉ Odos Thalita 17, Iraklio ☎ 28102 24012

ELECTRICITY

The power supply throughout Greece is 220 volts Ac, 50 Hz. Sockets are equipped for twin round-pin plugs. Some accommodation places in Crete have adapters, but visitors from Britain should bring an adapter and US visitors require a voltage transformer.

HEALTH AND SAFETY

- Crete is generally unthreatening and safe, but there can be exceptions.
- If you feel you have a genuine grievance against a service or facility, report the matter to the Tourist Police.
- If you are victim of, or witness to a crime contact the regular police.
- Medications that contain codeine are restricted in Greece. If you carry any such medications, although you are unlikely to be questioned, take an accompanying prescription.
- If you use prescribed medicines, however, it is advisable to carry a prescription record.

MEDICAL AND DENTAL TREATMENT

- Ask your hotel or letting agent for details of local doctors. Most resorts have a medical centre. Some popular resorts have very busy clinics.
- Hospitals: Venizelou Hospital ✉ Odos Knossou, Iraklio ☎ 28103 68000; University

Hospital ✉ Voutes (5km/3 miles south of city centre) ☎ 28103 92111; Rethymno General Hospital ✉ Odos Triandalydou 17, Rethymno ☎ 28210 27491; St. George's General Hospital ✉ Mournies (5km/3 miles) south of Chania city centre) ☎ 28210 22000.

- Dental treatment must be paid for. Make sure you have insurance cover.

OPENING TIMES

- Shops: daily 9–2, 5–9 in summer
- Museums and archaeological sites: daily 10–3; many have evening opening in summer. Some places stay open throughout the day and this is noted within individual entries.
- Offices: daily 9–5
- Banks: daily 9–2
- Pharmacies: daily 9–12, 5–6.30

POSTAL SERVICES

- There are post offices in all main cities, towns and some larger villages and at the larger resorts. Post boxes are yellow. Main post offices are often exceptionally busy; you may need to take a numbered ticket on entry.
- Iraklio ✉ Platia Daskalogianni 🕗 Mon–Fri 7.30–8, Sat 7.30–2
- Rethymno ✉ Odos Moatsou 21 🕗 Mon–Fri 7–7
- Chania ✉ Odos Peridou 10 🕗 Mon–Fri 7.30–8, Sat 7.30–2

TELEPHONES

To make a call from a street telephone you require a phone card, *telekarte*. These can be bought for a few euros at small local shops, souvenir shops and chiefly at street kiosks. Slot-in telephone cards are least value. Scratch number telephone cards can give you anything up to three hours of call time. Most mobile phones adjust to Greek service providers, although international calls can be expensive. It is worth buying a rechargeable SIM card while you are in Greece. Using a mobile phone while driving in Greece is prohibited.

ETIQUETTE

- It is impolite to make negative comments in public about the Greek religion, culture or the Greek State.
- Recreational drug use and supplying drugs of any kind is treated as a major crime in Greece and can result in very long prison sentences.
- Nude bathing is illegal in Greece, although some beaches have sections officially designated as naturist. Topless bathing is often the norm on many beaches, but local sensibilities should be respected off the beach and near religious institutions.
- Flash photography in churches and museums is often disapproved of. If you want to photograph a local person, ask their permission. Don't take photographs near military installations or of military personnel; Greek authorities are very sensitive about this.

PUBLIC HOLIDAYS

1 Jan New Year's Day; 6 Jan Epiphany'; Feb/Mar Kathari Deftera/Shrove Monday (41 days before Easter); 25 Mar Independence Day; Mar/Apr Holy Week Celebrations; 1 May Labour Day; 3 Jun Holy Spirit Day; 15 Aug Feast of the Assumption; 28 Oct Ochi Day; 25/26 Dec Christmas Day/St. Stephen's Day

Language

The official language of Crete is Greek. Many locals speak English, but knowledge of a few words of Greek is useful in rural areas where locals may know no English. It is also helpful to know the Greek alphabet—particularly for reading street names and road signs. Some useful words and phrases are listed below, with phonetic transliterations and accents to show emphasis. Because the method of translating Greek place names has changed recently, some spellings may differ from older ones you find on the island.

ACCOMMODATION	
hotel	*xenodhohío*
room	*dhomátyo*
...single/double	*...monó/dhipló*
for three people	*ya tría átoma*
can I see it?	*boró na to dho?*
breakfast	*proinó*
guest house	*pansyón*
toilet	*twaléta*
bath	*bányo*
shower	*doos*
hot water	*zestó neró*
balcony	*balkóni*
campsite	*kamping*
key	*klidhí*
towel	*petséta*

USEFUL WORDS AND PHRASES	
yes/no	*né/óhi*
please	*parakaló*
thank you	*efharistó*
hello	*yásas, yásoo*
good morning	*kalí méra*
good evening	*kalí spéra*
good night	*kalí níkhta*
I don't understand	*thén katalavéno*
goodbye	*....adío or yásas, yásoo*
sorry	*signómi*
where is...?	*poú eené..?*
help!	*voíthia!*
my name is...	*meh léne...*
I don't speak Greek	*then miló helliniká*
excuse me	*me sinchoríte*

EATING OUT

restaurant	*estiatório*
café	*kafenío*
menu	*menóo*
lunch	*yévma*
dinner	*dhípno*
dessert	*epidhórpyo*
waiter/waitress	*garsóni/servitóra*
the bill	*loghariazmós*
bread	*psomi*
water	*nero*
wine	*krasi*
coffee	*kafés*
tea (black)	*tsái*

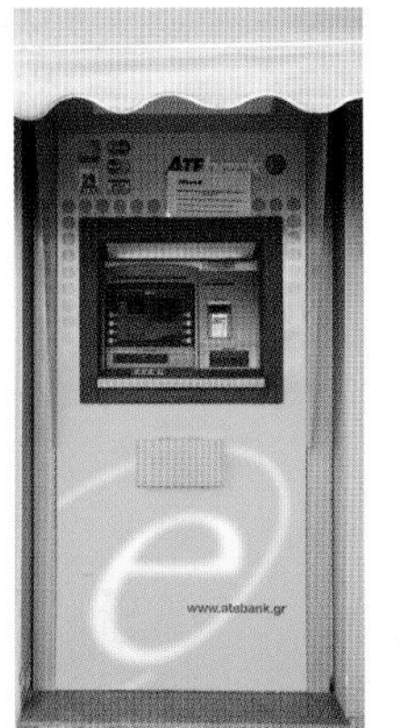

MONEY

bank	*trápeza*
exchange office	*ghrafío sinalághmatos*
post office	*tahidhromío*
money	*leftá*
cash desk	*tamío*
how much?	*póso káni?*
exchange rate	*isotimía*
credit card	*pistotikí kárta*
travellers' cheque	*taxidhyotikí epitayí*
passport	*dhiavatíryo*
can I pay by...?	*boró na pliróso me...?*
cheap/expensive	*ftinós/akrivós*

TRAVEL

aeroplane	*aeropláno*
airport	*aerodhrómio*
bus	*leoforío*
...station	*...stathmós*
boat	*karávi*
port/harbour	*limáni*
ticket	*isitírio*
...single/return	*...apló/metepistrofís*
car	*aftokínito*
taxi	*taxí*
timetable	*dhromolóyo*

Timeline

THE GREAT MAN

Eleftherios Venizelos (1864–1936) was Crete's most famous political figure, instrumental in achieving the island's final union with Greece, and then serving as Greece's Prime Minister and being credited as the 'maker of modern Greece'. Born in Mournies near Chania, he died in Paris—his grave overlooks Chania from a beautiful memorial garden.

DRESSED FOR HISTORY

History is stitched into the often everyday wear in Cretan mountain villages such as the *vraki*, black baggy trousers, tucked into *stivania*, knee-length boots, topped off by a black shirt and the famous *sariki*, a crocheted headscarf fringed with tiny knots.

From left: Ruins at Knossos; Grand Staircase, Phaistos; wall painting of the Turkish fleet; Venizelos's grave near Chania; monks' quarters, Moni Arkadiou; German War Cemetery, Maleme

7000–6000BC Crete settled by Neolithic hunter-gatherers, probably from Asia Minor.

3000–1800BC Minoan civilization. Construction of first 'palace' towns at Knossos, Phaistos, Malia and Zakros.

1450BC Minoan palaces and towns destroyed by unknown disaster. Mycaeneans arrive in Crete.

1370BC Final destruction of Knossos, possibly by Mycenaeans.

1100–67BC Dorian and Classical Greek society emerges in Crete.

67BC–AD395 Romans control Crete, during which time St. Paul introduces Christianity.

395–824 Crete ruled from Byzantium after Roman schism.

824 Andalucian Arabs take over Crete.

961 Byzantines retake the island.

1204–1669 Venetians control Crete, during which time they develop many of the island's towns, villages and fortifications.

1453 Constantinople falls to Ottomans. Refugees, including many accomplished artists, come to Crete.

1645 Turks capture Chania and Rethymno.

1669 Candia (Iraklio) surrenders to Turks who annexe the island after Venetians withdraw. Crete under Ottoman control for the next 229 years.

1821 Uprising against the Turks during the Greek War of Independence.

1866 Iconic sacrifice by several hundred Cretans in the explosion at Moni Arkadou.

1897 Great Powers of Europe take over Crete.

1898–1913 Crete as an independent entity.

1900 Sir Arthur Evans starts excavating Knossos. Federico Halbherr begins work at Phaistos.

1913 Crete becomes part of Greece.

1941–45 German occupation of Greece generates fierce resistance and brutal reprisals.

1960s Tourism develops as an industry.

1967–74 Dictatorship of Greek Colonels.

1986 Greece joins EU.

2010 Monetary crisis in Greece leads to unpopular financial reforms demanded by EU.

A TANGLED WEB

Crete suffered mightily under the Ottoman and German occupations, but the Venetians reacted every bit as nastily at the merest sniff of rebellion. They frequently burned whole villages in reprisals for rebellion and executed all able-bodied men and boys, often as a 'warning' against potential dissent.

PARADISE LOST

At some point of Minoan history–the date 1450 has long been identified–most of the Minoan palaces and towns were razed and destroyed by fire. This was roughly contemporaneous with the explosion of the volcano of Thira (Santorini), 142km (88 miles) north of Iraklio, which is believed to have rained down molten lava particles onto Crete and to have generated a massive tsunami. Other theories argue destruction over time by invading Mycenaeans or during internal civil wars.

Index

INDEX

TWINPACK
Crete

WRITTEN BY Des Hannigan
COVER DESIGN Catherine Murray
DESIGN WORK Lesley Mitchell
INDEXER Marie Lorimer
IMAGE RETOUCHING AND REPRO Jackie Street
PROJECT EDITOR Apostrophe S Limited
SERIES EDITOR Marie-Claire Jefferies

Colour separation by AA Digital Department
Printed and bound by Leo Paper Products, China

A CIP catalogue record for this book is available from the British Library.

ISBN 978-0-7495-6805-4

We have tried to ensure accuracy in this guide, but things do change, so please let us know if you have any comments at travelguides@theAA.com.

Published by AA Publishing, a trading name of AA Media Limited, whose registered office is Fanum House, Basing View, Basingstoke, Hampshire RG21 4EA. Registered number 06112600.

Front cover: AA/I Cumming
Back cover: (i) AA/I Cumming; (ii) AA/C Sawyer; (iii) AA/I Cumming; (iv) AA/I Cumming

A04027
Maps in this title produced from mapping © Freytag-Berndt u. Artaria KG, 1231 Vienna-Austria

The Automobile Association would like to thank the following photographers, companies and picture libraries for their assistance in the preparation of this book.

Abbreviations for the pictures credits are as follows – (t) top; (b) bottom; (c) centre; (l) left; (r) right; (AA) AA World Travel Library.

1 AA/I Cumming; **2/3** AA/I Cumming; **4t** AA/I Cumming; **4l** AA/I Cumming; **5t** AA/I Cumming; **5b** AA/I Cumming; **6t** AA/I Cumming; **6cl** AA/I Cumming; **6ccl** AA/I Cumming; **6ccr** AA/I Cumming; **6cr** AA/I Cumming; **6bl** AA/I Cumming; **6bc** AA/I Cumming; **6br** AA/I Cumming; **7t** AA/I Cumming; **7cl** AA/I Cumming; **7ccl** AA/I Cumming; **7ccr** AA/I Cumming; **7cr** AA/P Enticknap; **7bl** AA/I Cumming; **7bc** AA/I Cumming; **7br** AA/I Cumming; **8/9** AA/I Cumming; **10t** AA/I Cumming; **10tr** AA/K Paterson; **10cr** AA/I Cumming; **10br** AA/I Cumming; **10/1** AA/K Paterson; **11t** AA/I Cumming; **11tl** AA/K Paterson; **11cl** AA/P Enticknap; **11bl** AA/I Cumming; **12t** AA/I Cumming; **12tr** AA/I Cumming; **12ctr** AA/A Mockford & N Bonetti; **12cbr** AA/I Cumming; **12b** AA/I Cumming; **13t** AA/I Cumming; **13tl** AA/I Cumming; **13tcl** AA/I Cumming; **13cl** AA/I Cumming; **13bcl** AA/I Cumming; **13b** AA/I Cumming; **14t** AA/I Cumming; **14tr** AA/I Cumming; **14ctr** AA/I Cumming; **14cbr** AA/I Cumming; **14b** AA/I Cumming; **15t** AA/I Cumming; **15b** AA/I Cumming; **16t** AA/I Cumming; **16tr** AA/I Cumming; **16ctr** AA/I Cumming; **16cbr** AA/I Cumming; **16b** Lato Boutique Hotel; **17t** AA/I Cumming; **17tl** Lato Boutique Hotel; **17tcl** AA/I Cumming; **17bcl** AA/I Cumming; **17b** Copyright Cretaquarium-Thalassocosmos archives; **18t** AA/I Cumming; **18tr** AA/I Cumming; **18tcr** Brand X Pics; **18bcr** AA/I Cumming; **18b** AA/I Cumming; **19t** AA/I Cumming; **19ct** AA/I Cumming; **19cb** AA/I Cumming; **19b** AA/I Cumming; **20/1** AA/I Cumming; **24l** AA/I Cumming; **24tr** AA/I Cumming; **24br** AA/I Cumming; **25t** AA/I Cumming; **25bl** AA/I Cumming; **25br** AA/I Cumming; **26l** AA/I Cumming; **26c** AA/I Cumming; **26r** AA/I Cumming; **27l** AA/I Cumming; **27c** AA/I Cumming; **27r** AA/I Cumming; **28t** AA/I Cumming; **28c** AA/I Cumming; **28b** AA/I Cumming; **28/9** AA/I Cumming; **30t** AA/I Cumming; **30b** AA/I Cumming; **31t** AA/I Cumming; **31b** AA/I Cumming; **32** AA/I Cumming; **33** AA/I Cumming; **34** AA/I Cumming; **35** AA/I Cumming; **36** AA/C Sawyer; **37** AA/I Cumming; **40t** AA/I Cumming; **40c** AA/I Cumming; **40b** AA/I Cumming; **40/1** AA/I Cumming; **42l** AA/I Cumming; **42r** AA/I Cumming; **42/3** AA/I Cumming; **43t** AA/I Cumming; **43b** AA/I Cumming; **44l** AA/I Cumming; **44r** AA/I Cumming; **45l** AA/I Cumming; **45c** AA/I Cumming; **45r** AA/I Cumming; **46** AA/I Cumming; **47t** © imagebroker/Alamy; **47bl** AA/I Cumming; **47br** AA/N Hicks; **48l** AA/I Cumming; **48r** AA/I Cumming; **49l** AA/I Cumming; **49c** AA/I Cumming; **49r** AA/I Cumming; **50t** AA/I Cumming; **50b** AA/I Cumming; **50/1** AA/I Cumming; **51t** AA/I Cumming; **51b** AA/I Cumming; **52l** AA/I Cumming; **52r** AA/I Cumming; **53t** AA/I Cumming; **53bl** Getty Images/Gallo Images/Travel Ink; **53br** AA/I Cumming; **54t** AA/I Cumming; **54b** AA/I Cumming; **55t** AA/I Cumming; **55bl** AA/I Cumming; **55br** AA/I Cumming; **56t** AA/I Cumming; **56b** AA/I Cumming; **57t** AA/I Cumming; **57b** AA/I Cumming; **58t** AA/I Cumming; **58b** AA/K Paterson; **59** AA/I Cumming; **60** AA/I Cumming; **61** AA/I Cumming; **62** AA/I Cumming; **63** AA/I Cumming; **64** AA/I Cumming; **65** AA/I Cumming; **66/7** AA/C Sawyer; **68** AA/C Sawyer; **69** AA/I Cumming; **72l** AA/I Cumming; **72r** AA/I Cumming; **73l** AA/I Cumming; **73r** Copyright Cretaquarium-Thalassocosmos archives; **74t** AA/I Cumming; **74b** AA/I Cumming; **74/5** AA/I Cumming; **76l** AA/I Cumming; **76r** AA/I Cumming; **76/7** AA/I Cumming; **77t** AA/I Cumming; **77bl** AA/I Cumming; **77br** AA/I Cumming; **78l** AA/I Cumming; **78r** AA/I Cumming; **78/9** AA/I Cumming; **79t** AA/I Cumming; **79b** AA/I Cumming; **80l** AA/I Cumming; **80r** AA/I Cumming; **81t** AA/I Cumming; **81bl** AA/I Cumming; **81br** AA/I Cumming; **82t** AA/I Cumming; **82bl** AA/I Cumming; **82br** AA/K Paterson; **83t** AA/I Cumming; **83bl** AA/I Cumming; **83br** AA/I Cumming; **84** AA/I Cumming; **85** AA/I Cumming; **86** AA/C Sawyer; **87** AA/I Cumming; **90/1** AA/I Cumming; **91t** AA/I Cumming; **91b** AA/I Cumming; **92l** AA/I Cumming; **92r** AA/I Cumming; **93l** AA/I Cumming; **93r** AA/I Cumming; **94l** AA/I Cumming; **94r** AA/N Hicks; **95l** AA/I Cumming; **95r** AA/I Cumming; **96l** AA/I Cumming; **96/7t** AA/I Cumming; **96/7b** AA/I Cumming; **97** AA/I Cumming; **98t** AA/I Cumming; **98bl** AA/I Cumming; **98br** AA/I Cumming; **99t** AA/I Cumming; **99bl** AA/I Cumming; **99br** AA/I Cumming; **100t** AA/I Cumming; **100bl** AA/I Cumming; **100br** AA/I Cumming; **101** AA/I Cumming; **102** AA/I Cumming; **103** AA/K Paterson; **104** AA/I Cumming; **105** AA/I Cumming; **106** AA/C Sawyer; **107** Lato Boutique Hotel; **108t** AA/C Sawyer; **108tr** AA/I Cumming; **108tcr** Elounda Beach Hotel; **108bcr** AA/K Paterson; **108b** AA/I Cumming; **109** AA/C Sawyer; **110/1** AA/C Sawyer; **112** AA/C Sawyer; **113** AA/I Cumming; **114-120t** AA/I Cumming; **120b** European Central Bank; **121t** AA/I Cumming; **122t** AA/I Cumming; **122c** AA/I Cumming; **122b** AA/I Cumming; **123t** AA/I Cumming; **123tr** AA/I Cumming; **123cl** AA/I Cumming; **123br** AA/I Cumming; **124t** AA/I Cumming; **124bl** AA/I Cumming; **124br** AA/I Cumming; **124/5** AA/P Enticknap; **125t** AA/I Cumming; **125bl** AA/I Cumming; **125bc** AA/I Cumming; **125br** AA/K Paterson.

Every effort has been made to trace the copyright holders, and we apologise in advance for any accidental errors. We would be happy to apply any corrections in the following edition of this publication.